THE MOST BEAUTIFUL CHINESE MINDS SERIES

"最美中国人"丛书

ENTREPRENEURS: STRIVING FOR HAPPINESS

创业者：幸福是奋斗出来的

"最美中国人"丛书编委会 编著

Sinolingua
华语教学出版社

First Edition 2022
Third Printing 2023

ISBN 978-7-5138-2194-0

Published by Sinolingua Co., Ltd
24 Baiwanzhuang Street, Beijing 100037, China
Tel: (86)10-68320585, 68997826
Fax: (86)10-68997826, 68326333
http://www.sinolingua.com.cn
E-mail: hyjx@sinolingua.com.cn
Printed by Beijing Hucais Culture Communication Co., Ltd.

Printed in the People's Republic of China

“最美中国人”
丛书编委会

前言

“最美中国人”丛书以中英对照的形式向外国读者讲述新时代中国人民的奋斗故事。本丛书用细致生动的笔触介绍了志愿者、创业者、90后、普通百姓和老年人这几个不同人群中的典型故事，反映出中国人民在中国共产党的领导下实现全面小康的逐梦历程。丛书一共五册，分别是《志愿者：让爱传递到每个角落》《创业者：幸福是奋斗出来的》《出彩90后：我的青春不后悔》《平凡老百姓：把日子过出精气神儿》《中国“传家宝”：那些可爱的老人们》，每册包含八到十个真实故事。为了让外国读者更加直观地了解中国社会的发展和人民生活的巨大变迁，丛书除了文字故事之外，部分故事还配有视频二维码，读者扫描二维码即可观看与文章配套的人物故事视频。

FOREWORD

"The Most Beautiful Chinese Minds" is a book series for international readers featuring stories of Chinese people from all walks of life in today's China. Presented in both Chinese and English, the series reveals the vivid and personal stories of the everyday lives of volunteers, entrepreneurs, post-90s youth, ordinary people and senior citizens as they strive to realize their own dreams and the national dream of building a moderately prosperous society in all aspects under the leadership of the Chinese Communist Party. The series includes five volumes: *Volunteers: Making the World a Better Place*, *Entrepreneurs: Striving for Happiness*, *Born in the 90s: Never Regretting Our Youth*, *Ordinary People: Living a Vibrant Life*, and *Charming Seniors: Keeping Up with the Times.* Each volume consists of eight to ten true stories about real people. It is a must-read for those wishing to better understand the true experiences of everyday Chinese people in today's China and the remarkable changes taking place in their lives. We have also provided QR codes for some stories which can link to online videos about the people from the passages.

目录 | CONTENTS

90 后小伙儿的“柿业情缘”

Guo Jiaming and His Tomato-cultivation Career

作者：王　晨　孙　玥
翻译：雷雅妮　李红霞

90 后小伙儿的“柿业情缘”

90 后小伙儿郭佳明在 2016 年把碱地柿子（柿子：当地人对西红柿的俗称——编者注）种植项目带回家乡辽宁省盘锦市，成立了盘锦菜根堂农业科技有限公司。从此，他开启了“柿业”之旅——种植碱地柿子，带动周边农户发家致富。

现在，郭佳明将公司经营方向从西红柿种植拓展到技术帮扶、育苗育种、成果销售等多方面，公司占地面积从 4 亩发展到 16 亩，2019 年营业额达到 600 多万元，带动当地农户 300 余人，形成了碱地柿子“产—学—研”经营模式。

在他的温室大棚里，一株株半米多高的西红柿秧挂着红彤彤的果，长势喜人。“碱地柿子肉厚、味甜、多汁爽口，钙和维生素 C 的含量都超过普通西红柿。”郭佳明介绍，不是所有柿子都叫碱地柿子，只有在盐碱度为 0.3‰ 到 1.5‰ 的盐碱地种植，甜度在

8～12 度，外观达到一定标准时，才可以被称为碱地柿子。

靠钻研的劲头取得种子生产资质

为了不断完善碱地柿子的种植技术，郭佳明不满足于自家实验室的科研成果，他虚心学习先进技术和优秀经验；为了获得碱地柿子的种子生产资质，郭佳明多次前往上海一家农科院，希望借助科技实验室培育出优良的种子。他邀请专家来盘锦实地考察，“我们需要能适应当地环境的良种，确保没问题了，才会推广给当地农户。”

这家农科院针对盘锦当地环境，历时两年研发出了几类西红柿品种。但拿到了种子并不意味着成功。种子种下后，一开始生长得并不理想。郭佳明只能沉下心来找原因。郭佳明回忆，为了挑选良种，需要设置对照组，长期观察记录数据。寒冬时节，温室大棚里的温度能达到 30 多摄氏度，为了减少对照误差，他一天至少要在大棚里待 6 小时。

授粉对于西红柿的结果率影响很大，

当前很多农业基地多使用进口蜂授粉。郭佳明团队通过对蜜蜂成活率、工作量的综合考察，最终选定熊蜂作为授粉蜂。

郭佳明说："我跟农户们说，有坑我先跳，我们先用熊蜂看能不能行。但是当初因为实验用熊蜂的数量太少，最后还是托了朋友，才搞到了几箱熊蜂。经过一年的生产观察，农户们也认可了熊蜂，今年我们就会推广。"

在盘锦市，菜根堂是第一家申请种子生产资质的公司。由于缺乏资质办理的经验，郭佳明的申请一度陷入停滞。最后，郭佳明想到：寿光是全国大型蔬菜集散中心，我们是不是可以去取取经？

于是，郭佳明多次往返于盘锦和寿光。通过借鉴寿光的申办经验，并积极与当地农业局和政府部门沟通，2020 年 4 月，他们取得了"碱地柿子"的种子生产资质。

2019 年年初，碱地柿子的技术和运营就已经成熟，郭佳明却开始了新的"折腾"。他和公司的技术团队开办"农民夜校"，为种植碱地柿子的村民免费义务开展技术培训和政策解读。“夜校的课程设置是受我参加的‘青马’培训班的影响。我们为农民讲解相关农业政策，帮助他们了解自己的权益；同时将线下实践和理论授课相结合，让农民能够真正学到种植技术”。

夜校兴办之初，郭佳明和团队满怀干劲儿，在当地利用村广播、横幅、摆摊等多种宣传模式向村民介绍课程。但村民一看到郭佳明和技术员都那么年轻就不禁摇头。“很多村民种了一辈子地，看我们年纪这么小，第一反应就是不信任”。

夜校招生受挫，郭佳明并没有气馁。他带着技术员，跟着村干部一家家走访西红柿种植农户，介绍课程，宣传“科学种植”理念。他还邀请农户来生产基地参观。看着一台台先进的设备仪器，试验田里的西红柿长势喜人，就有村民动了心。最终，郭佳明的夜校课程吸引了50多名学员。学员从一开始半信半疑，到后来干劲儿满满。

除了亲自上阵分享经验，郭佳明和公司技术员还和一些农业专家通过网上连线为农户进行场外教学，并将课堂延伸到了田间，实打实地为农户解决种植问题。

西红柿丰收了，很多农民兴奋地找到郭佳明，“今年柿子每亩增产了近10%，没想到种地也有这么多学问”。

郭佳明说：“参加培训班的学员当年都增收5000元到10000元。”

让种植模式变得“高大上”

在郭佳明的带动下，当地的种植模式变得“高大上”了起来。种地不再是耕地、播种、施肥的老路子，而是要先给土地做一个“体检”，对土地进行土壤检测。根据“体检结果”，进一步确定种植方式是用碗栽培还是田间培育，还能为不同的土壤提供配方式的施肥和用药。

为了方便检测和研发，郭佳明咬牙投资了20多万元，兴建了公司自己的实验室，能够满足农业检测的基本需求。郭佳明说：“受到‘用工业的标准去做农业’的启发，我们很重视数据支撑，这样后期才能依据科学规律种植。”

但一开始，村民对此并不认可，认为是“花架子”。对此，郭佳明利用培训和夜校授课的机会，向村民科普科学种植的重要性，免费为农民提供土壤速测。

郭佳明说：“其实农民很实在。因我们的种植经验而受益的农户都很快接受了科学种植的理念，还帮助我们进行科普宣传。”

郭佳明笑称：“虽然农业盈利很慢，但是家里人都挺支持的。只有爷爷一开始不太理解，他当了一辈子农民，觉得好不容易我们能离开土地了，结果我又回来种地。看到大家认可、政府支持，爷爷也能理解我了。我想让种地不再是苦累活儿，让农民更轻松地挣钱。”

Guo Jiaming and His Tomato-cultivation Career

Guo Jiaming is a twenty-something entrepreneur from the city of Panjin in northeastern China's Liaoning Province. In 2016, he introduced an agricultural project to his hometown—growing tomatoes in alkali soil. He formed a company called Panjin Caigentang Agricultural Science and Technology Co., Ltd. This was the start of his career growing tomatoes in alkali soil. He works together with local farmers, and they have been making a fortune.

Currently, Guo's business range now extends beyond tomato-growing into such areas as technical support, seedling and breeding, and marketing. The floor space of his company has increased from roughly 29,000 to 115,000 square feet. In 2019, sales reached more than six million yuan. It has helped drive the local economy, and more than 300 local farmers have benefited from the project. As a result of this great success, the "growing—learning—research" management model was formed focused on growing tomatoes in alkali soil.

In his greenhouses, the half-meter-high stalks are thick with red tomatoes. "Tomatoes grown in alkali soil are thick, sweet, and juicy, with more calcium and vitamin C than ordinary tomatoes," said Guo. "Not all tomatoes can be called alkali-soil tomatoes. Only those grown in soil with a saline-alkali content between 0.3‰ and 1.5‰ can be called alkali-soil tomatoes. They must also have a sweetness level between 8 and 12 and an appearance that meets a certain standard."

Obtaining Seed Production Qualifications Through Unremitting Perseverance

Unsatisfied with the research results from his own laboratory, Guo maintained an open mind in order to improve his cultivation technology. With the goal to acquire the production qualifications of alkali-soil tomatoes, he visited an academy of agricultural sciences in Shanghai several times, hoping their facilities and expertise could help him cultivate quality seeds. He also invited academy experts to Panjin for a field study. "What we needed were fine seeds which could adapt to the local environment. Only after that goal had been achieved could we distribute the seeds to the local farmers."

After over two years of research, the academy finally developed several varieties of seeds. However, simply developing fine seeds did not equate to success. In fact, after the seeds were planted, they didn't grow well at first. Guo forced himself to be calm and find a solution. He came to the conclusion that a control group needed to be set for long-term observation and data-recording. Even in the cold winter, the temperature in the greenhouse could reach over 30°C, but in order to record accurate data he had to stay there for at least six hours a day so that comparison errors could be minimized.

Pollination is vital to the growth rate of tomatoes. Nowadays, many agricultural bases will use imported bees for this task. Through a comprehensive study on the survival rate and productivity of different types of bees, Guo's team finally chose bumble bees to finish the pollination.

Guo said, "I told the local farmers I would be the first to see if it was feasible to use bumble bees to pollinate tomatoes. We were short of bumble bees for our experiments, so I asked friends to help me find some, and we finally got a few boxes. After a year of production and observation, the farmers grew so satisfied with the bumble bees that we're going to do it on a larger scale this year."

Guo's company was the first in Panjin to apply for the seed production qualification for alkali-soil tomatoes. However, his lack of related experience led to his application being stalled. It eventually occurred to him that they could go to Shouguang (a city in Shandong Province in eastern China) since it was a large national vegetable distribution center.

Guo made several trips between Panjin and Shouguang. He learned the application procedures of Shouguang and actively communicated with the local agricultural bureau and other government departments concerned. Finally, in April 2020, Guo acquired the production qualification for alkali-soil tomato seeds.

At the beginning of 2019, as Guo was still pursuing the production qualification for his seeds, he was also thinking of a new project. He established a "Night School for Farmers" to offer free technical training and policy interpretation for all the local alkali-soil-tomato farmers. "The curriculum of the night school was modeled after what I'd learned in my Young Marxist Class. We introduced to them related agricultural policies to help them understand their own rights and interests. The courses also included both classroom learning and farm work to help the farmers grasp the tomato-growing skills."

At the very beginning, Guo's team worked hard to publicize their courses, using such methods as village broadcasts, banners and setting up stalls. Nevertheless, most villagers ignored Guo and his team due to their young age. "For farmers who had been growing crops their whole lives, they determined we were too young to be trusted."

Although few people enrolled in the night classes, Guo did not give up. He personally went out with technicians and village officials to introduce the courses to local farmers, and to disseminate the concept of "scientific growing". He also invited the farmers to visit his production bases. Seeing the advanced facilities, instruments and the well-grown tomatoes, the farmers started to become convinced. Ultimately, more than 50 students were enrolled in the night school. Though they were dubious at first, by the end they were full of enthusiasm.

Besides sharing their own personal experiences with the farmers, Guo and his technicians were able to set up online meetings between the farmers and agricultural specialists who could help the famers tackle difficulties they were having in the fields.

After a successful harvest, many farmers told Guo that their tomato yields had increased by nearly 10%, and that it had never occurred to them growing tomatoes required so much expertise.

Guo said, "For those who attended the night school, their income increased by 5,000 to 10,000 yuan that year."

Growing the Planting Model

Guo continues to update and improve his tomato-growing model.

Farming is no longer the old way of simple "ploughing, sowing and fertilizing". Instead, the soil needs a "physical examination"—a test of the soil quality first. The test results will not only determine which planting model to choose—bowl-cultivated or field-nurtured—but will also provide targeted fertilization and pesticide plans according to the different soil characteristics.

In order to facilitate better testing and research, Guo invested more than 200,000 yuan to build their own laboratory. "We're inspired by the idea of using industrial standards to conduct agricultural production. We attach great importance to data support so that our tomato-growing meets all current and best scientific methods."

In the beginning, however, villagers did not approve of this, considering it too "fancy". This was why Guo began the evening classes, to impart to the farmers the importance of using scientific methods to grow their produce. He even provided quick soil tests for them for free.

"The farmers are very pragmatic, actually," Guo said. "Those who benefited from our planting experience accepted the notion of scientific planting very quickly, and they were the ones to help us popularize it."

Guo smiled. "Despite the slow profit return, my family still chose to support me. As a lifetime farmer, only my grandfather didn't understand at first why I returned home to go into farming when we had so many seemingly better options. But later on, after seeing the approval by the villagers and the government's support, he finally came around. My goal is to make farm work less of drudgery and help farmers earn money more easily."

Scan for a Video

从“豆腐西施”到“创业盟主”

From a Tofu Maker to a Startup Champion

作者：王培莲
翻译：张景艳　龚　艳

从“豆腐西施”到“创业盟主”

“做豆腐，用得着上大学吗？”2009年，从长春大学电子信息工程专业毕业的卜睿不想找工作，决心要回农村老家做豆腐，父母听说后火冒三丈，邻里、亲戚也议论纷纷。

可卜睿偏偏认为，“做传统手工豆腐、树品牌，大有商机”。她设想：开豆腐加工厂，把生产扩大到传统作坊的100倍；坚持手工制作，开门店，打造“卜家豆腐”品牌。

如今，卜睿的设想已一一实现。她注册成立了吉林省昌睿食品有限公司，目前年销售额500万元。除了水豆腐、干豆腐和豆浆等豆制品，公司还发展经营黑猪和土鸡养殖等业务，卜睿还发起成立了“长春市女大学生返乡创业联盟”。在这个被大家称为“豆腐西施”的姑娘看来，“农村创业大有前景”。

“我做的豆腐与众不同”

卜睿出生在长春市英俊镇胡家村，家里几代都做豆腐营生。大三那年，她在网上看到一个男孩因长期误食含有“吊白块”的豆腐而罹患尿毒症的新闻。渐渐地，她萌生了毕业后用祖传手艺制作绿色豆腐的想法，“在外上学时，吃到的豆腐都没有家乡的味道”。

俗话说，人生有三大苦行业——打铁、撑船、做豆腐。干这行，晚上就要进作坊，磨浆、熬浆、点脑、上包、压包，一套流程下来就到了第二天凌晨4点，天一亮就得准备去早市销售。

“活儿累，赚钱又不多。”一开始，卜睿的父亲卜精昌很难理解女儿的选择，辛苦供她上大学走出了乡村，她学成后却要回头走他们的老路。

“因为我做的豆腐与众不同。”别家的干豆腐按斤卖，卜睿做的则按张销售。令同行和顾客佩服的是，卜睿手工做的干豆腐每一张重量都一样，薄而有韧性。一张干豆腐切成10多米的长条，展开拉成圆圈，4个人拉住，还可以保持不断。

创业之初，卜睿只是按部就班做传统手工豆腐，每天早上6点去早市销售。但没多久，她发现每张干豆腐的薄厚不一样，增加了很多称重的时间。“早上太忙，每次这样添称很麻烦。”

卜睿动起脑筋：能不能做出每张重量一样的手工干豆腐？母亲蒋素环听后笑了，“煎饼有论张卖的，还没听说过干豆腐也论张卖”。

要让干豆腐薄厚均匀，就得保证每次舀出的豆腐脑重量必须一致。父母告诉卜睿，以他们几十年的手艺都很难达到这种要求。

架不住卜睿的软磨硬泡，母亲决定尝试一下。可练了十多天，还是没成功。母亲有些埋怨地对卜睿说，人不是机器，不可能每次舀出的浆子都一样重。但卜睿还是不甘心。母女俩又坚持练了两个月，奇迹出现了。凭借招牌干豆腐和纯正的卤水豆腐，两年内卜睿就开了3家门店。

不断折腾，与小作坊拉开距离

想把豆腐生意做大，与小作坊拉开距离，就得扩大生产规模。虽然卜睿攒了点儿钱，但要重新选址建厂还差30万元。卜睿没想到，为了给自己凑钱，父母居然瞒着她卖了用来养老的回迁楼。

“家人倾其所有支持我，我必须得做好。”卜睿准备大干一场。2011年下半年，正规、标准的新厂房建好了，每天可以产上万斤豆腐，是小作坊产量的100倍。这样的生产规模，却让不少同行看起了热闹，“这么多豆腐卖给谁？”

“热闹”不止于此，卜睿又继续投资10万元，给豆腐注册了“卜家”的商标，还申请通过QS质量认证。卜睿说：“不能等机会来了才想着提高自己，要做好充分准备，商机一来，随时可以抓住。”

无意中一次看报，卜睿发现了重要商机：吉林省很多大企业和单位的食堂采购豆制品困难，当时几乎没有企业能够提供QS质量认证的豆腐，产量也少。

“我可以把各大单位食堂作为目标客户。”因为卜睿生产的豆腐有QS质量认证，很快她就与吉林大学达成了合作，负责供应吉林大学23个食堂的豆腐。开门红后，卜睿又陆续和长春多家中小学签约。2012年，她的豆腐销售额一下增长到300万元。

喜欢琢磨的卜睿还为每天做豆腐产生的大量豆渣找到了“消耗对象”——黑猪。

一次在山区的同学家吃饭，卜睿发现同学家里饲养的黑猪是没经过改良的纯种黑猪，吃粮食长大，养一年才出栏，“只用白水煮这种黑猪肉，吃起来就很香”。

后来她了解到，这是东北传统的荷包猪，非常稀少，是进入高端肉制品市场的优良品种。由于养殖时间长，养黑猪的人少，卜睿费了很大劲儿才找到13只小猪。为保持品种纯正，她要求自繁自养，3年内只养不卖。

养猪的时候，卜睿又动起脑筋：很多人爱吃带大理石花纹的雪花牛肉，会不会也有雪花猪肉呢？为了找答案，她分别把猪养到不同月份宰杀。一直养到第16个月时，惊喜出现了，瘦肉里终于出现了大理石花纹。

卜睿的“新花样”在市场上大受欢迎。在2014年举办的长春农博会上，“卜家”黑猪肉一周内销售额就达10万元。黑猪肉的生产和销售也成为公司创收的又一个重要来源。

发起成立女大学生返乡创业联盟

如今，卜睿的企业从最初30平方米的小作坊发展到占地面积4000平方米的厂房，产品从豆制品发展到黑猪肉、土鸡、土鸡蛋等多种农产品，销售渠道也从早市发展到与多家大企业和学校合作，开门店、进驻大型超市等。她的企业还先后解决了当地农村100多名剩余劳动力的就业问题。

这几年，经常有人在网上看到有关卜睿的报道，慕名来讨教做豆腐的手艺，卜睿都会毫无保留地分享。现在，已经有一些大学毕业生被吸引加入卜睿的企业，和她一起在农村创业。

2015年，卜睿发起成立了“长春市女大学生返乡创业联盟”，有27名创业女大学生加入。大家互通有无，分享销售渠道。联盟还为很多成员争取到清华大学、北京大学、义乌电商培训机构等学习机会。

把联盟打造成连接城市和乡村的枢纽是卜睿的初衷。在她的规划里，创业者可以用新知识、新技术和新模式帮助和引导村民生产优质、安全的农产品，再通过互联网将农产品销往全国各地。

From a Tofu Maker to a Startup Champion

“Why did you bother to go to college if you wanted to make tofu?” Bu Rui’s parents were furious at their daughter’s decision to make tofu, or bean curd, in their home village instead of finding a job in a big city, as most graduates do. Bu Rui, a graduate of Electronic and Information Engineering at Changchun University, became the talk of the village because of her choice.

However, Miss Bu insisted that there was great business potential in traditional handmade tofu if she could build her brand. Her vision had two parts: one was to start a tofu factory with a production capacity 100 times that of traditional workshops; the other was to set up stores selling her handmade food under the brand “Bu’s Tofu”.

All of her dreams have come true. Her Jilin Changrui Food Co., Ltd. registered annual sales of 5,000,000 yuan. Apart from bean products, such as soft tofu, dried bean curds, and soya-bean milk, the enterprise boasts more operations like raising black hogs and free-range chickens. Bu also launched a startup alliance for female graduates back in Changchun City. In the mind of this beautiful tofu maker, there is great promise in rural areas.

“The Tofu I Made Is Different”

Bu’s family has been making a living on tofu for generations in Hujia

Village, Yingjun Town, Changchun City. During her junior year, she read news of a boy who contracted uremia from tofu that contained rongalit. Bu then had the idea of making healthy tofu using the craft she inherited from her family after graduation, since she "never ate tofu as delicious as the homemade tofu during my college years".

As a Chinese saying goes, there are three tiring trades in the world — being a blacksmith, punting, and making tofu. Tofu making means working through the night, including soya-bean grinding, boiling, coagulation, packaging, and squeezing. The process is usually finished at 4 a.m. when it is almost time for fresh tofu to come into the market.

"More pains, fewer gains," Bu's father admonished. It was almost impossible for him to accept his daughter's choice to follow his hard trade as she could have better chances outside the village, which was what he had expected of her after all those years of education.

"But I can make better tofu," she responded. True to her claim, Bu's dried bean curds can be sold by sheets instead of by weight. To the amazement of her peers and customers, every sheet of Bu's dried bean curd is as thin, flexible, and heavy as one another. Each can be sliced into a thin strip over ten meters long and strong enough to be stretched into a circle without breaking.

In the beginning, she followed the routine of traditional tofu making and went to the market at six a.m. every day. However, it didn't take her much time to find that every tofu sheet varied in thickness, resulting in more time to weigh it. "It's very troublesome during the busy morning hours," she said.

One day, an idea struck her: was it possible to make dried bean curd sheets of equal weight? Her mother dismissed the idea with a laugh, "It's possible for thicker pancakes. But for tofu? No way!"

Even distribution of jellied bean curd was essential to produce dried bean curd sheets of the same thickness. She was told it was impossible, even for workers as skilled as her parents.

Overwhelmed by Bu's pestering requests, her mother decided to give it a shot. But attempts for ten days proved to be a failure. Her mother grumbled that people couldn't distribute the soya-bean milk as precisely as a machine did. But with Bu's persistence, their experiment became a success two months later. In two years, Bu opened three shops selling specialty tofu sheets and brine tofu.

Persistent Attempts Lead to Great Development

It is necessary to expand production to boost the business, as a sharp contrast with smaller workshops. But even with her savings, 300,000 more yuan was needed to build a new factory. To her surprise, her parents raised the money by selling the apartment they planned to retire to.

"I will try every means not to let down my family, who has wholeheartedly supported me," she said. By the latter half of 2011, a factory was built, with an output of five thousand kilograms a day, 100 times that of the smaller workshops. Such expansion roused sarcasm among her peers: "How could so much tofu be sold?"

But Bu didn't stop there. With another investment of 100,000 yuan, she registered the trademark "Bu's Tofu" and obtained QS certification.

As she put it, "Opportunities are for prepared minds. I must be ready."

Occasional reading of the newspaper brought forth a great business opportunity: many large enterprises and public institutions in Jilin Province found it difficult to purchase soybean products for their canteens due to inadequate production of producers with QS certificates.

"Such canteens could be my target consumers," she decided. Backed by her QS certification, she reached an agreement with Jilin University to supply tofu for its 23 canteens. A good beginning is half done. Before long, she signed contracts with many primary and middle schools in Changchun, and her tofu sales hit three million yuan in 2012.

She even managed to find "target consumers", black hogs, for the huge amount of bean dregs.

On a visit to her classmate living in a mountainous area, she found that the black hogs bred there were purebred species. Such hogs fed on grain and needed to grow for a year before they were ready for the market. "Their meat is delicious, even with simple cooking," she described.

Later, she learned that such rare black hogs from northeast China were the best choice for the high-end meat market. Great efforts had been made before she managed to get 13 piglets to raise due to their rarity. Three years were spent for the hogs to reproduce without a single hog for sale to keep the bloodline pure.

With a resourceful mind, Bu began to wonder: marbled beef has been popular, then what about marbled pork? Her solution was to slaughter the hogs at different periods in their lives, and, finally, her trials paid off – there was marbled pork in hogs at 16 months old.

This new type of meat was much sought after in the market and earned her 100,000 yuan in a week at the Changchun Agricultural Expo in 2014. Since then, the black hog breeding has become an important source of revenue for her company.

The Launch of Startup Alliance for Female Graduates

Today, her original workshop of 30 m^2 has developed into a factory of 4,000 m^2, and a variety of products are available, such as quality pork, free-range chickens, and eggs. The marketing channels are diversified through cooperation with large enterprises and universities, and added up with stores and supermarkets. Moreover, her enterprise has provided over 100 jobs in local villages.

Online reports about Bu Rui brought her lots of followers, for whom she never refrained from sharing her skills in making tofu. And now, some college graduates have joined her company to work in the rural areas.

Bu launched Startup Alliance for Female Graduates in Changchun in 2015 with 27 participants. All the members learn from each other and share marketing channels. The alliance managed to find the members opportunities for further studies in training programs at Tsinghua University, Peking University, Yiwu e-commerce training center, and more.

Bu's initial ambition was to build the alliance into a bridge between urban and rural areas. The members, relying on their new knowledge, skills, and models, can help villagers produce and sell their safe and quality products across the country.

Scan for a Video

当中华白姜遇上学艺术设计的小姐姐

From a Designer to a Ginger Farmer

作者：王海涵　王　磊
翻译：李冰青

当中华白姜遇上学艺术设计的小姐姐

每天，26 岁的安徽铜陵创业青年胡婷婷都会来到工厂，与白姜“亲密接触”。她要看看工人的生产情况，检查产品制作流程和包装、发货、库存情况，还要接待不少慕名前来参观的年轻人。

“只有和产品待在一起，我才有思路和灵感。我每天都要琢磨如何拓展销售渠道，产品如何迭代，让白姜从形式、功能、种类上创新，真是操碎了心。”胡婷婷感慨道。

她的创业项目和工厂位于铜陵佘家大院村，背靠青山，四周环绕着树林、竹林，面积约 200 平方米。工厂设计风格文艺清新，更像是一个工作室。佘家大院村是铜陵白姜的特色产地，铜陵白姜因姜嫩皮白而得名，品质上乘，有“中华白姜”之美誉。北宋年间，铜陵白姜被列入朝廷贡品。其加工制作技艺是“安徽非物质文化遗产”，2019 年入选全球重要农业文化遗产预备名单。

从学艺术设计的小姐姐，到面朝黄土背朝天的姜农，胡婷婷已经习惯了农业创业的艰辛，“我们目前白姜种植面积4亩左右，每年的产量约1万斤，收购农户生姜1万斤。希望明年能翻倍。”

有困难算什么？我偏要种生姜

从小在佘家大院村吃着白姜长大，胡婷婷对白姜有着特殊的情感。

“大院村土质肥沃、气候适宜，特别适合生姜生长。铜陵姜农有独特的栽培、加工技艺，加工后的白姜晶莹透明，芳香四溢，脆嫩爽口。”胡婷婷介绍，铜陵姜农的栽培绝活独具特色，是全世界独有的技术。

大学毕业后，胡婷婷在成都工作。在一次家庭聚会上，长辈们告诉胡婷婷，因为技术要求高又太苦太累，秉持古法种植生姜的人越来越少，再过十年，或许就没人会种白姜了。

据了解，铜陵白姜产业规模化、集约化水平及创新能力不足，导致产业发展“后劲不足”。

不想让延续两千多年的白姜文化慢慢被遗忘，胡婷婷决定跟父母学习种白姜，让白姜迸发新的活力。

她觉得，长辈们销售白姜的方式传统且原始，就是直接卖掉地里长出的生姜，这无法提升铜陵白姜的附加值，也无法让消费者深刻感受白姜深厚的文化底蕴。

2018年，她正式辞去工作，返乡创业的第一件事就是“拥抱”姜田。但是把身份完全转变成“农民”，胡婷婷可花费了大力气。第一次下地的她，就被锄地这个基本功给难倒了。

种生姜的锄头比一般锄头更重，女孩子一般抡不起来，胡婷婷使用锄头的姿势也不是特别正确。夏天天气炎热，没干一会儿，胡婷婷就累得精疲力尽，手掌也被磨出了水泡。

更大的阻碍来自村民和父母。看到在田里干活儿的胡婷婷，来往的人总时不时议论几句：“一个小姑娘上班上得好好的，干吗要回来种地，是不是在公司混得不好？做农业能有什么出息？”

作为村里第一个考上大学的人，胡婷婷肩负着家人很大的期望。她的父母不明白，为什么女儿要放弃高薪工作，回来做这么苦的事。“但我从来没想过放弃，我认定自己的创业路，就要种生姜。”胡婷婷说。

“我从长辈身上学到，做农业需要极大的耐心。每年，生姜产出只有一季，却要花全年的时间来悉心料理，同样的动作和工作流程要重复多次。”胡婷婷每天都要去姜田观察生姜生长状况，看看水分够不够，光照够不够，有没有病虫害……往往回来以后衣服上都是泥巴，夏天衣服会汗透几遍。

光有耐心和毅力还不够，玩转互联网思维

胡婷婷的父母种了一辈子生姜，凭手艺和经验吃饭。胡婷婷跟在父母后面，记录白姜种植的完整过程，详细了解需要注意的细节，梳理出相关量化数据。经过近一年的反复实践和观察，胡婷婷总算掌握了一些古法种植技术。

父母被女儿的执着所打动。他们开始传

授一些宝贵经验给女儿，比如对于时令、天气的把握。

“老一辈种姜人养成了靠身体感知大自然湿度、温度变化的习惯，而我只会看天气预报。”胡婷婷介绍，父母会判断天气，在头天晚上或第二天清晨干农活儿前就做好相关准备和预案，来决定农业生产该怎么进行、怎么实时调整，这让她受益匪浅。

2018年9月初，胡婷婷悉心照料的生姜收获了，她形容：“感觉像自己孩子出生一样高兴！”

生姜种出来了，开拓销售渠道也是个难题。刚开始，胡婷婷到处找亲戚、朋友、同学去推荐产品，但这些力量远远不够，她需要更多渠道和新客户。

“种地靠体力，销售、推广考验脑力。只要遇到有意愿的客户，我们都会磨破了嘴皮子介绍，想方设法让他们尝一口。很多人对新兴的品牌并不感兴趣，我们就把产品免费送给他们试吃，只要有一个回头客，我们都非常开心。”胡婷婷说。

如何在同类产品中体现差异化，她摸索

出来一条路子：从艺术设计的角度去“重构”一款农产品，让产品像一个艺术品、工艺品或者“礼物”；同时要让人充满想吃的欲望，吃了还想吃，吃完还想分享给其他人，真正打动消费者。

2018年10月，胡婷婷的老公程陵也返乡了，帮她一起创业。他结合所学新媒体制作与开发知识，为产品设计、后期运营、品牌形象出了不少点子。

平时，程陵还会剪辑、制作短视频，开发小程序，让受众增强对白姜的体验感。很多创意，夫妻俩会一起讨论、交流。尽管也有意见不一的时候，但二人经过“争吵”，会很快达成一致，“这和做艺术设计一个道理，反复打磨才能出精品。”

经过反复磨合，他们将创业品牌取名“山礼”，将产品比喻成“大自然馈赠的礼物”。“第一篇微信公号推文发出后，阅读量竟然有5000多，评论区很多留言都鼓励我们坚持下去，传播铜陵白姜文化，给我们鼓劲儿。”胡婷婷回忆。

那段时间，胡婷婷经常熬夜设计产品包

装，反复修改。有趣的包装和创新的传播思路使她的创业产品脱颖而出，第一个月就获得20万元的销售额。此外，她还做电商，开淘宝店，尝试微店和小程序，让白姜产品插上互联网的翅膀。

让人们在吃的同时感知传统文化

“我身边搞农业创业的青年越来越多，但大家普遍面临推广等难题。”创业3年多来，一些铜陵本地年轻人返乡，加入胡婷婷的创业团队。目前，核心成员5个人都是90后，大家有着共同的目标：改变人们对于生姜的固有认知，让人们在吃的同时感知传统文化。

白姜种植受自然条件影响大，且古法种植技术要求严苛，一不小心就会让白姜染上瘟病，导致减产，这也是胡婷婷目前面临的另一个痛点。

“我们和姜农合作，收购生姜作为原材料，并从村里挑选制姜高手到工厂工作，带动当地就业。”胡婷婷希望能带动更多年轻人学习种植白姜，助力乡村振兴。

在每年秋天生姜收获的季节，胡婷婷会特地将村里50岁到75岁左右的制姜手艺人集中请到工厂，帮助制姜，以确保生产质量。老制姜手艺人也很乐意前来帮忙，看到村里年轻一辈认认真真种生姜，他们十分欣慰。

“我们的白姜只在晴天制作、加工，确保至少3个小时的阳光照射，所有的白姜都是纯人工手撕出来再装瓶腌制，需要花费很大的时间成本和人工成本。”胡婷婷介绍，自己只选用原产地佘家大院的生姜，用完全的古法工艺进行手工制姜，不会添加任何添加剂，并且有自己独到的腌制配方，这些都有别于市场上一般的白姜加工工艺。

此外，胡婷婷还吸收一些村里的剩余劳动力来厂里做工，从事包装等工作，让他们有事可做。

“未来，我们要让更多人了解生姜，让大众知道，我们年轻人也愿意且能种好生姜。”胡婷婷梦想着自己的品牌能让铜陵白姜文化发扬光大，让白姜走出大院，走出铜陵，走向世界。

From a Designer to a Ginger Farmer

Every day, 26-year-old Hu Tingting comes to her ginger factory in Tongling County, Anhui Province to look after her white ginger. She checks the daily production quality, ginger processing procedures, packaging, shipments, and storage. She also meets young people who come to visit her factory.

"I have to be here every day to get inspiration and ideas about how to develop existing marketing channels, how to improve the product, and how to produce better ginger that is more appealing," Tingting says with an exhausted expression.

Tingting is the CEO of her own ginger factory in Shejia Dayuan Village of Tongling County, and is surrounded by trees, bamboo, and hills. Instead of being a traditional factory, it looks more like an art studio. Shejia Dayuan Village is actually well-known for its special kind of white ginger which is famous for its white peel and freshness. People consider it China's best white ginger because of its superior quality. During the Northern Song Dynasty (960 – 1127), Tongling White ginger was presented as a tribute to the emperor. White ginger processing techniques have been included in Anhui Province's Intangible Cultural Heritage List and were later included in the 2019 Global Agricultural and Cultural Heritage List.

From an art designer to a ginger farmer working in the field, Tingting is already used to the hardship of starting an agribusiness. "Currently our cultivation area is about four *mu* with a production of 5,000 kilos per year. We also purchase 5,000 kilos of ginger from other farmers. I'm hopeful that production will double next year."

No Matter How Hard, I Must Plant Ginger

Growing up in Shejia Dayuan Village and eating white ginger since she was little, Tingting has always had a special affection for white ginger.

"The fertile soil and nice weather here is very suitable to grow ginger. Tongling ginger farmers have special planting and manufacturing techniques. Pickled ginger is almost translucent with a nice flavor and crispy taste," Tingting says. "The cultivation skills of Tongling ginger farmers are unique in the world."

After graduating from university, Tingting went to work in Chengdu. Once in a family gathering, Tingting's elder relatives told her that because ginger planting was very tiring and had strict planting requirements, fewer people planted ginger using the time-honored cultivation techniques. They said that perhaps after ten years no one would plant white ginger anymore and those traditional techniques would be lost.

It is understood that the Tongling white ginger industry is very hard to develop and may gradually disappear because of the small factory scale, lack of innovation, and inefficient production methods.

Not wanting to see this tradition which has lasted for more than two thousand years disappear, Tingting decided to study ginger planting from her parents in order to revitalize this old tradition.

She felt the way villagers sold ginger was a bit primitive and lacked a good sales strategy. The absence of brand storytelling failed to add more commercial value to the product and didn't tell consumers of the enduring history of Tongling's ginger cultivation.

In 2018, Tingting decided to quit her job as a designer and return to her hometown to develop her own ginger business. But it was difficult to shift from a designer to a farmer since Tingting knew nothing about farming, and did not even know how to use a hoe.

Even worse is that the hoe used for planting ginger is heavier than a normal hoe, which makes it even harder for a young woman to handle. The way Tingting hoed was not quite right, either. After a day of working she was exhausted, with blisters on her palms.

However, bigger obstacles came from local villagers and her parents. Seeing her work in the fields, people commented, "Why on earth would a girl leave her design company to come back home to farm? Maybe she didn't do well in the company. But what can she achieve by planting ginger?"

As the first college student in the village, Tingting's family had high expectations for her. Her parents didn't understand why she gave up her well-paid job to return home to become an exhausted ginger farmer. "Though many people opposed my decision, I never thought about giving up. I made up my mind that I must plant ginger."

"I learned from my parents that I needed to have great patience to be a ginger farmer. There is only one ginger harvest season per year, but farmers need to spend the whole year constantly checking its progress and taking good care of it." Every day, Tingting went to the fields to check if the ginger had enough water, sunshine, and to look out for pests. Her clothes were often stained with mud. In summer, her clothes got wet from sweat.

Patience, Perseverance, plus the Internet

Tingting's parents are experienced, life-long ginger farmers. Tingting observed her parents and documented the complete process of white ginger cultivation, learning about the important details that needed attention, and summarizing relevant quantitative data. After nearly a year of observation and practice, Tingting finally mastered some traditional ginger-planting techniques.

Touched by her persistence, Tingting's parents gave their full support, and taught her important tips, such as how to deal with seasonal changes and weather.

"The older generation of ginger farmers can actually sense changes in humidity and temperature with their bodies, but I still need to look at the weather forecast." Tingting explained that her parents could adjust their planting plan and determine how agricultural production should be carried out in the evening or before the morning based solely on their early judgments of the next day's weather. This amazing ability benefited Tingting greatly.

In early September 2018, Tingting's ginger was harvested, and she described it as "feeling as happy as if I had given birth to my own child!"

Even though the ginger was successfully planted and harvested, it still had to be sold, and this was a big problem. At first, Tingting asked her relatives, friends, and classmates to help her promote her products, but this was not enough. She needed more sales channels and new clients.

"Planting depends on physical strength, while marketing requires brainpower. As long as there were clients interested in our products, we could get them to take a bite. For people who were not interested in a new brand like us, we gave out free samples. Every time we got a repeat client, we were very happy."

Tingting also came upon a great marketing strategy to differentiate her white ginger from other similar products. She utilized her past experience as a designer to "reconstruct" ginger as a work of art to make it more attractive to customers which would make them want to buy it, eat it, and share it with people.

In October 2018, Tingting's husband Cheng Ling returned home to help her with the business. Using his knowledge of media production, he gave great advice on product design, media operations, and brand image building.

Cheng Ling also made short videos and developed apps to let customers know more about white ginger. There were many such ideas the couple would usually discuss together, and although arguments would sometimes occur, the two would ultimately reach an agreement. "It's just like art design. You have to repeatedly refine your artwork to make it better."

After numerous discussions, the couple named their brand "Mountain's

Gift" since they believed that white ginger was a precious gift given by nature. "Our first WeChat blog post hit more than 5,000 views. Many viewers left their comments and encouraged us to keep developing our ginger business and pass on this old planting tradition to more people." Tingting recalled.

During the initial marketing stage, Tingting spent many nights up late retouching her packaging designs, but it was all worth it. Her inspirational marketing strategy and interesting packaging won her a sales revenue of 200,000 yuan in the first month. She also took advantage of e-commerce where she operated an online store on Taobao and other online platforms.

Eating and Experiencing Traditions

"There are more and more young people engaged in agricultural entrepreneurship, but they're having difficulties in product promotion and other practical issues," Tingting says. Over the past three years, young people have been returning home to join Tingting's ginger business. At present, each member of her core team was born in the 90s, and their common goal is to change people's concept of ginger and inform them of this old ginger-planting tradition.

At the same time, growing ginger is no easy task. The white ginger plant is greatly affected by natural conditions, and the traditional planting technique has strict requirements. Any slight oversight may lead to crop illness and a reduction in overall yield.

"We cooperate with ginger farmers by purchasing raw ginger from them, and then we invite ginger experts in the village to work in our factories to process it." Tingting has said she hopes her business can inspire younger generations to learn ginger planting which would in turn help promote local employment and economic development.

During the autumn harvest season, Tingting invites experienced ginger craftsmen of the village to her factory to help process the ginger and ensure the production quality. The old ginger craftsmen are willing to help, and they are very glad to see the younger generation in the village continuing to plant ginger.

Tingting's ginger processing is totally different from other white ginger processing techniques. Tingting explains, "We only process ginger on sunny days, and we make sure the ginger is dried under direct sunshine for at least three hours. All the white ginger is manually torn out and then bottled and pickled, which costs a lot of time and labor." According to Tingting, she only uses ginger cultivated in Shejia Dayuan Village, and completely follows the traditional handmade ginger processing methods using her own unique curing formula and without adding any additives.

Tingting has also helped local people in the village by providing jobs like packaging, etc.

"In the future," Tingting says, "more people will know about our ginger and also that we are a young generation that is willing and able to grow ginger." Hu Tingting dreams that one day she can bring her ginger cultivation culture to a bigger stage and ultimately appear on international markets.

Scan for a Video

80 后白领夫妻小镇创业记

The Undertaking of a Young Couple

作者：先藕洁　许 译
翻译：薛彧威

80 后白领夫妻小镇创业记

一张简易的长木桌、一面灰色砖墙，墙上挂着几串干玉米和干辣椒加以点缀——这是80后小伙高玉楼的家，位于云南省丽江市华坪县荣将镇。两边围起来的竹栅栏，是高玉楼的妻子王娇砍竹子制作的。

2018年4月，夫妻二人开始在这个简单搭建起来的拍摄区制作短视频，之后在“快手”上发布。他们给自己的账号取了一个诗意的名字，叫“乡野丽江娇子”。王娇负责出镜，高玉楼负责拍摄及后期制作，内容主要以家乡风景、乡野美食为主，有时还会在视频中销售农特产品。视频发布不久就吸引了大量粉丝，如今涨到200多万。

现在，他们一个月卖农特产品能有3万多元的销售额，其中通过“快手”拍视频售卖的农特产品占总销售额的一半以上，同时也带动了村里数十户村民增收。

在此之前，这对小夫妻是在城市打拼的

上班族。从公司白领到返乡创业青年，他俩内心经历了不少挣扎。

从公司白领到返乡创业青年，他们经历了什么？

2010年，高玉楼和王娇两人在昆明上同一所大学，高玉楼的专业是建筑景观设计，王娇和他一个系，学的是数字媒体设计。身为宣传部长的高玉楼经常组织社团成员开展活动，王娇则是其中一员。两人对彼此印象都不错，很快这对年轻人开始热恋。

2014年，大学毕业后，王娇进入一家设计公司，做了一名3D动画师，月薪5000元左右。而高玉楼在一家装修公司做设计师，月薪最多的时候有七八千元。对于生活节俭的王娇和高玉楼来说，这样的工资水平足够他们过“小资生活”，每个月还能存不少钱。

2016年，高玉楼和王娇结婚，和大多数上班族一样，两人过着朝九晚五的规律生活。直到有一天，高玉楼在一款视频类的手机软件上看到一个视频，一位水果商户正在直播卖樱桃，直播间很多人都在问如何购买。高玉楼陷入了沉思：家乡的芒果那么好，是不是也可以试试以这种方式推销？高玉楼萌生了返乡创业的想法。

当王娇知道丈夫想放下在昆明已打拼好的一切、回到家乡用视频直播卖芒果时，她坚决反对。王娇说，最让她焦虑的是对未知的担忧，做返乡“吃螃蟹的第一人”去直播卖水果，没法预测这背后要承担的风险。

高玉楼的家乡是素有“晚熟芒果之乡”美称的丽江市华坪县。之前高玉楼就曾有过返乡卖芒果陪家人、用所学知识建设家乡的想法，所以当看到通过直播来销售的方式时，高玉楼心里返乡创业的愿望就更加强烈了。

一开始，王娇不断劝丈夫放弃返乡创业的想法，两人也曾为这件事争吵过好几次。高玉楼理解妻子的担忧，他决定先回乡尝试一下，证明给妻子看。

在离开昆明之前，高玉楼和几位朋友一起设计了装芒果的纸箱，回乡后开始到华坪县各个芒果园实地考察，记录拍照，收集资料。7月份正是芒果成熟的季节，高玉楼开始尝试第一次视频直播。他在自家的芒果园里，一边向收看直播的观众介绍芒果的品种、口感，一边从树上摘新鲜的芒果放到纸箱里。

“当时直播间有很多人问这些芒果的产地、价格、购买方式，我一边回复他们的问题，一边加对方微信填订购信息。”高玉楼说。让他没想到的是，20分钟就销售出三箱芒果，与以往花费人力、物力到小镇市场上销售的方式相比，效率提高了很多。高玉楼特别开心，直播结束后立刻给对方发货。高玉楼通过直播方式销售芒果，2016年销售额达20多万元。

2017年，高玉楼和嫂子一起又开始直播销售芒果，这次比上一年的成绩好，3个月就达到40多万元的销售额。除此以外，高玉楼还帮助周边63户果农扩展销路，其中有23户都是建档立卡的贫困户。通过两年时间，王娇看到高玉楼的努力和成绩。王娇认为丈夫确实有这方面的天赋和能力，也抓住了互联网的机遇。于是，2017年，王娇同意和丈夫一起返乡创业。同年他们有了一个女儿，小名叫“小豆芽”。

种芒果、拍美食，淳朴的小镇生活吸粉百万

两人辞职返乡创业，身边的朋友有支持的，也有反对的。返乡后，王娇和高玉楼确实遭遇到不少困难。

高玉楼打算经营一个“快手”短视频账号，通过拍摄视频增加粉丝，同时通过销售芒果来增加收入。但第一个引起关注的视频却是女儿带来的。

“当时我在做一道青椒鱼的菜，我一岁多的女儿小豆芽知道我在做饭，就帮我把鱼端了过来。”说到第一个在“快手”这个短视频平台上引起关注的热门视频，王娇说她也没想到女儿的无意入镜会引来大量粉丝关注，并且当天这个视频的播放量就高达96万。

2018年，芒果收获的季节，他们拍摄了一个为女儿制作芒果酱面包的视频，视频的结尾还增加了一个简短广告，如果想买芒果就加主页上的微信。没想到的是，这次尝

试吸引了大量的粉丝和购买者。剪刀面、汤猪脚、龙猫饼干……王娇做了很多制作美食的视频，因为她有美术功底，所以在美食的色彩搭配上也很擅长，很多粉丝留言夸赞王娇的厨艺，也有粉丝想知道高玉楼的拍摄技巧。

接着，两人差不多每隔两天就会发布一个美食视频，粉丝从最初的几十到如今的百万。随着粉丝群的日益壮大，两人也受到家乡很多人的关注。慢慢地，镇上很多年轻人开始向高玉楼夫妇学习，平时大家聚集在一起交流，请教视频拍摄的制作方式。

拍视频的同时，还要种植芒果，高玉楼家的芒果园一共有2000棵果树，大约20亩左右。高玉楼有种植芒果的经验，但王娇没有。“种植芒果要做很多繁琐的工作，而且天气非常炎热，从做设计跨行到种植，真的感觉很辛苦。”王娇说。但是芒果上市时，王娇又会觉得特别有收获。对于现在的她来说，之前在大城市时没有看到这个地方的优点，当真正地融入这个氛围，发现这里的生活环境很轻松，人情味也很浓。

发展自身之外帮助贫困户脱贫 未来准备开一家食品公司

每年7到10月芒果成熟，夫妻俩就通过视频卖芒果，剩下时间就卖其他的水果、农特产品。这几天，他们在筹备帮隔壁村的一家贫困户卖蜂蜜。这对贫困夫妻都已经50多岁，男主人叫张兴文，他的妻子有精神障碍，女儿正在上高中，全家的经济来源全靠他一个人。他有30多年的养蜂经验，但是没时间去销售蜂蜜，囤积了大量蜂蜜放在家里，每个月都入不敷出。高玉楼夫妇目前正在筹备的就是帮张兴文卖蜂蜜，帮助他增加收入。

说到未来再远一点儿的规划，王娇说将来想开一个无添加的食品公司，让更多的人吃到健康美味的家乡美食，同时也宣传物产资源丰富的家乡。“从小在家乡的一花一木陪伴之下成长，离开家乡后会经常牵挂着。我就想回乡创业，争取为家乡做出贡献，推动家乡发展。”

The Undertaking of a Young Couple

A simple, long wooden table. A gray wall with bundles of dried corn and pepper. This is the home of thirty-something Gao Yulou. The house is located in the town of Rongjiang, near the city of Lijiang in Yunnan Province. It is flanked by bamboo fences built by Gao's wife, Wang Jiao.

In April 2018, the couple began shooting short videos at this simple set and uploading them to Kuaishou, an online short video platform. They gave their account a poetic name, "Beauty of Rural Lijiang". Wang usually appears in the videos while Gao is in charge of shooting and post-production. The videos mainly feature local scenery, rural cuisine, and special agricultural produce of the area. Not long after they began this project, the videos began attracting a lot of followers. They currently have surpassed two million subscribers.

They currently generate more than 30,000 yuan a month by selling special agricultural products. Over half of these sales come directly from viewers of their Kuaishou channel. They have also helped boost the incomes of many households in the village.

Prior to this, the young couple used to work in the city. From white-collar employees to rural entrepreneurs, the two have experienced many struggles.

Making a Difference

In 2010, Gao and Wang were studying at the same university in Kunming. Gao majored in architectural landscape design and Wang was in the same department majoring in digital media design. As the head of the publicity organization of the university, Gao would often arrange activities for members, and Wang was among them. The two got a good impression of each other and soon fell in love.

Upon graduation in 2014, Wang entered a design company and became a 3D animator with a monthly salary of around 5,000 yuan. Gao found a job with a decoration firm as a designer and earned around 7,000 - 8,000 yuan per month. For this pair who were used to living quite frugally, their incomes were not only enough for a comfortable life, but also enabled them to save a lot.

The two got married in 2016. Like most office workers, they lived a regular nine-to-five life until one day when Gao chanced upon a video on a mobile phone app. In the video, a fruit seller was promoting his cherries in a live video stream, and many people were asking how they could buy them. Suddenly, Gao was lost in thought: The mangoes in my hometown were very good. I wondered if I could sell them in a similar way? He started to harbor the idea of returning home to start a new business.

After telling his wife his idea to give up everything they had in Kunming and return home to sell mangoes on live video, she raised strong objections. Wang said that the one thing that concerned her most at that time was the unknown. She did not like the idea because there would be unpredictable risks involved, and they could not foresee the outcome.

Gao's hometown is actually famous for its mangoes, and has long been dubbed "home of late-maturing mangoes". His idea to return home and sell mangoes also included spending more time with his family and also thinking of ways to build up his hometown with the knowledge he had acquired. After seeing the novel "live-stream" selling method, his wish only grew stronger.

In the beginning, Wang Jiao tried very hard to persuade her husband to give up his idea, and they had many arguments about the matter. Gao was well aware of his wife's concerns. He decided to return home first to give it a try to prove it could be done.

Before leaving Kunming, Gao and a few friends designed a cardboard box to carry the mangoes. After coming back to Huaping, he went to many mango orchards to conduct field research, and collected data by taking notes and photos. Then, when it was time for the harvest, Gao made his first live stream broadcast. He introduced the mangoes to the audience while picking them from the trees and putting them into boxes.

"During the live stream, many viewers were asking about the growing region, price and how to place an order. I answered their questions and added their WeChat contacts to fill in the order information." Gao recalled. To his amazement, three boxes of mangoes were sold within 20 minutes. Compared with the traditional way of selling them at the town market which could cost a lot of manpower and material resources, this method was much more efficient. Overjoyed, Gao mailed the goods to his customers immediately after the broadcast.

Through live streaming, his sales reached over 200,000 yuan in 2016.

The next year in 2017, Gao did the live stream again along with his sister-in-law. The result was even better than the previous year. Mango sales amounted to more than 400,000 yuan within just three months. In addition to the good sales, Gao was able to help 63 nearby fruit growers expand their sales channels. Among these, 23 were poor households. Two years had passed, and Wang Jiao had witnessed her husband's efforts and achievements. She realized that he had the potential to do this well and had grasped this unique opportunity brought about by the growing power of the internet. In 2017, she agreed to leave Kunming and run their new business together with her husband. They had their daughter that year, whose nickname is "Little Bean Sprout".

A Simple Lifestyle Attracts Millions of Fans

When others heard about the couple's decision to return home and start the new undertaking, they received both support and opposition. They encountered many obstacles at the initial stage.

Gao's original plan was to open a Kuaishou account and attract followers by making short videos, so as to push his mango sales and thus increase income. It never occurred to him that the first video to attract the most attention would be of their daughter.

"I was making a green pepper fish dish. My over one-year-old daughter knew that I was cooking dinner, so she brought the fish over to me." Wang never expected that the child's sudden appearance in the video would get so many hits— 960,000 views in just that day!

During the 2018 mango harvest season, the couple produced a video describing how to make mango jam bread. A short ad was added at the end: "Anyone interested in buying mangoes, please do not hesitate to reach us through the WeChat account on our home page." To their surprise, this new attempt also attracted lots of fans and buyers. They made more videos cooking different dishes: "scissors" noodles, trotter soup, Totoro biscuits.... Wang Jiao not only acted in many cooking videos, but also applied her design skills to the color arrangement of each dish. A lot of followers left messages praising her cooking techniques, while some others were eager to learn Gao's filming skills.

The two would upload a video almost every three days, and the number of subscribers increased from several dozen to the current one million or so. With their growing number of fans, the couple began attracting more attention within their hometown. Gradually, many young people in town began learning from them and they often gathered together to discuss ways of shooting and making videos.

While making videos, they also continued to care for their mango orchard. There are 2,000 trees in Gao's orchard, covering an area of about 3.3 acres. Compared with her husband, Wang had no experience growing mangoes. "To plant mangoes, a lot of work needed to be done," Wang recalled. "The weather was very hot, and it was such a difficult task for me to transform from a designer to a fruit grower." But once their mangoes went to market, she felt the reward of her hard work. When living in the big city, she didn't see the advantage of living in a small town like this. But now fully integrated into rural life, she's realized the benefits. Life was relaxed, and there was a stronger human connection between people.

Future Plans

When the mangoes mature each July to October, the couple make new live stream videos to sell them. For the rest of the year, they sell other fruits and local specialties. Recently they have been preparing to help a poor family in the neighboring village sell honey. The couple are both in their 50s. The husband is Zhang Xingwen, who is the sole earner for the whole family. His wife has some mental disorders, and his daughter is a high school student. Zhang has more than 30 years' experience raising bees, but has no time to sell the honey. He has a huge stock surplus but can hardly make ends meet every month. Gao and his wife are making plans to help him increase his income.

When asked about their future plans, Wang said she wanted to set up a company selling additive-free food so that more people could enjoy the produce of their small town, which was both healthy and delicious, and let more people know about their hometown which was rich in natural resources. She said, "I grew up with flowers and trees in my hometown, and I've missed it so much ever since I left home. It has been my wish to go back one day and make contributions to the development of my own hometown."

Scan for a Video

返乡创业青年让乡土文化实现价值

Homecoming: Realization of Chinese Rural Culture

作者：邢　婷
翻译：李冰青

返乡创业青年让乡土文化实现价值

中郝峪村是个位于山东淄博大山深处的小村庄，距城区30余公里，绵延的群山阻隔了村庄与外界更多的联系，也一度阻断了全村360名村民的致富梦。没有人料到，这个村庄日后竟会与“股份”“公司”这些字眼相连。

给山村带来巨变的是青年“领头雁”赵胜建和他的9人管理团队。这群看上去不起眼的本土青年摸索出一条乡村发展与治理的新路。

“分”与“合”的智慧

2006年，大专毕业的赵胜建重返家乡，成为村里唯一一名常住的年轻人。

当年21岁的他不是没有告别大山的机会。毕业时，身为校学生会主席的赵胜建荣获“省级优秀毕业生”称号，面对的是踏入知名企业和出国深造等诸多选择。玫瑰色的前途触手可及。然而，这一切被一封家书打破：身为村支书的父亲突患严重心脏病，急需照顾。作为家中独子，赵胜建别无选择。

当时，中郝峪村的多数村民仍“靠天吃饭”，种植玉米、小麦，收入微薄。经过一番考察，心有不甘的赵胜建开办了一家桔梗加工厂，带领百名本村和邻村村民苦干，渐渐地，产品远销韩国，每年居然能盈利几十万元。此事给了赵胜建极大触动：农村不乏商机，关键看有没有闯劲儿。

这一边，正当赵胜建将事业经营得风风火火时，那一边，村里潜伏多年的发展危机日益显露。

自2003年起，村两委决定发展旅游致富。最初有6家“农家乐”，高峰时达30多家。随着数量增多，相互压价、争抢客源等恶性竞争时有发生，最终导致大半“农家乐”歇业，旅游致富这条路似乎越走越窄。

对省内外“农家乐”的一番考察却让赵胜建认准了其中的商机。如何走出多年来中国农村、农民和农业发展中“分分合合”

的怪圈，让习惯个体分散劳作的村民真正开始抱团闯市场却又不必付出一“合”就降低效率的高昂代价，重建市场背景下的乡村秩序，令他苦思。

赵胜建提出了大胆设想：以公司化集体运营方式，联合所有“农家乐”业户，把全村的土地、房屋等资源按评估办法整合入股，村两委兼任董事会成员，决定公司发展方向。至于分红，老弱病残不需投资即可享受无风险的人头股(capitation stock)，其他村民除了享受人头股外，还根据入股额度享受利润分成。

在这盘大胆的棋局中，土地悄悄进入市场交易程序：村民的责任田可以每分地1000元作价入股；一些村民承包村集体的山坡地等，按市场价评估入股；土地上的附着物，譬如桃树、板栗树等，按不同直径予以补偿。入股的土地可用来种植花卉、苗木，建立采摘园，甚至还可以让城里人通过网络平台“认领”，由村民帮忙种植。

在赵胜建看来，“就是把死的东西盘活”。

“让每个村民入股，这叫啥事？”

“现在都吃不饱，成立公司干吗？”

村民的质疑纷纷砸向这个年轻人。如何让村民心甘情愿地交出资产自愿入股？村委会同样顾虑重重。

倔强的赵胜建写下保证书，按下手印：自己投资，赚钱大家分，赔钱自己扛。他由此扛起了全村人的致富梦。

公司成立后，首要工作是拉客源。背着大捆宣传材料，赵胜建频频往返于周边城市，吃了无数闭门羹，中郝峪村的名气终于一点一点大了起来。

尚存的十七八家“农家乐”业户抱着试试看的心态，勉强入股。公司对其进行统一管理、统一定价、统一翻新，“我们只需要操心服务质量和卫生。”首批入股的李兴兰说。

一年后，首批入股业户全部收入翻番，旁观的村民们终于坐不住了，纷纷入股。至2014年，全村已有90家“农家乐”业户。

由“分”而“合”，股份制的实行，让

村民们真正意识到“来的都是客”，不论吃住在谁家，赚的钱全村人都有份，村民开始享受合作带来的红利。

而此时的“合”仍不乏“分”的影子，即充分鼓励和尊重每户“农家乐”的经营特色。每户“农家乐”根据整体档次，依照地方旅游部门的标准评定不同星级。每家的招牌也不一样，有的靠窝窝头味道正宗，有的靠山野菜品种齐全，有的靠煎饼口感劲道，还有的靠特色招牌饺子。

过去中郝峪村村民人均年收入不到2000元，如今人均收入达4.5万元。人头股则由最初时的90多元涨至4000多元。所有村民的合作医疗和养老保险均由公司承担，不少村民连续3年将拿到的分红一次次重新入股。

让乡土文化实现价值

完成股权制引入的同时，赵胜建开始思考如何为家乡量身定制一条独特的发展路径。在生硬嫁接工业文明和重新审视乡土文明之间，赵胜建毅然选择了后者。

没有单调的标语口号，如今一走进村口，中郝峪村以乡村情趣为主题的墙画就会扑面而来，堪称一大景观。从包饺子的每道工序到小孩夏天上树掏鸟窝，皆丝丝入扣，生动入画，勾起人们美好的回忆和向往。每隔几户，便会看到手捧特色美食的农家大娘形象，画面色彩浓郁，人物栩栩如生。二妗子馍馍坊、马大娘豆腐坊、老梁煎饼坊……这些美食招牌无形中成为全村的地标，吸引游客流连忘返。

在赵胜建看来，乡村游若想获得长足发展，硬件软件缺一不可，而所谓软件，就是最纯粹的乡土文化与乡土记忆。

“过去我们从没想过家门口的空气、环境，还有每家每户的拿手农家菜居然还能卖出一个好价钱。”郑芹兴奋地说。

在不少游客眼中，复活的农家厨艺与物件动人心弦：一中年游客眼含热泪，连续几小时在鏊子前摊煎饼，逝去母亲的记忆不断喷涌；参加夏令营的小学生们则从门牙和大牙的生动比喻中认识石碾和石磨的功用。

十多年来，在中郝峪村，被激活的不仅仅是远去的乡土文化，还有一度丧失效力的村规民约。

在中郝峪村公司化运营的图景中，村容村貌等公共秩序即公司营业环境，维持公共秩序成为公司成员即每位村民恪守的义务，村务由此成为公司事务。

这里的村规民约对乱扔垃圾、散养家畜、酗酒闹事等有着详细、严苛的规定，一旦违规，经其他村民举报，将在年底的人头股中扣除相应罚款。

公司对农村经常出现的不孝行为也有制约。按照村规：对不孝敬老人的儿女，只要老人找到村两委一次，其本户的全年福利将转发给老人。一个真实案例：一位八旬老人因两个儿子常年对自己不闻不问，不得已告到村委会，年底分红时，两个儿子的人头股全部转发给老人。

甚至赵胜建本人也被罚过钱。一天深夜，一位邻村朋友醉酒后在他家门前吼了一嗓子。规定既出，无人侥幸，年底分红时，他的人头股被扣除100元。

“这几年，大家手里有钱了，更在乎面子了。”赵胜建说，近一两年已鲜有村民被罚。

乡土文化在激活的同时，也悄悄得到了提升。如今走在中郝峪村，每家每户都基本建起了水冲式厕所，对接城市文明，让城里人在这里常住也没什么不习惯。前些年还偶尔看到的北方农村惯有的柴堆乱放、晾晒大粪等杂乱场景，经这几年旅游文明的“熏陶”，早就没了踪影。村道整洁有序，一条小河纵贯全村，流水潺潺，岸边杨柳依依，环境怡人。

每家每户墙上挂着的村规民约已直抵村民内心，并成为自觉。赵胜建对自己偶遇的一幕至今记忆犹新：一位游客随手将雪糕包装纸扔在地上，村里一个五六岁的小男孩儿发现后，立马跑上前捡起包装纸投入垃圾箱。

受益的不仅是村民，还包括村委会。如今村集体每年收入300多万元，相比于之前每年几千元的村集体收入，这笔钱意味着可投入更多公共事务。

为解决村里老人的后顾之忧，减轻儿

女们的负担，公司于2014年新建养老院，共设28个床位，全村70周岁以上的老人自愿入住，所有生活费由村委及公司各承担50%。为避免墓地乱占地，公司利用村里一块闲置菜地设立公墓，无偿提供给过世村民。

村里的疗养院正在紧张筹建中。赵胜建的这一想法孕育于父亲的病榻前，他希望让全村人享受到更优质的医疗服务。

引回本土的凤，共筑大家的巢

在中郝峪村委副主任陈焕富眼中，村里这十多年来的变化可谓“翻天覆地”。接下来怎么走，能走多远，还得靠人。

赵胜建不止一次为这个问题困扰过：十多年来，他尝试过从外面聘请专业管理人才，可最终一个也没留住。“后来仔细一想，还是个人利益至上，对这里没有感情。”赵胜建琢磨着怎么能把村里在外打拼的年轻人吸引回乡。

“在电话里，我就给他们‘画饼’。”赵胜建笑称。2010年，王佐接到赵胜建的电话后，立马辞去机床操控工作回了家乡。“家乡发展得越来越快，需要我们做些事情让它变得更好”。

这些年来，王佐见证了路灯从无到有，见证了家乡巨变，也见证了一个个童年玩伴陆续返乡。

开拓市场、餐饮服务、设计运营……这帮年轻人各司其职。在赵胜建的带领下，CS俱乐部、拓展训练营地陆续成立；村子有了微信公众号，别具一格的墙画跃上墙壁。他们甚至鼓捣着建树屋，在街边屋前安装欧洲小城流行的花箱。

年轻人的归来无疑给村子带来无穷活力。村民们不止一次撞见这帮年轻人围坐在房间里，热火朝天地讨论着村庄发展大计。

为了让公司的年轻团队汲取更多知识养分，赵胜建从北京、山东的高校请来十几位旅游管理、市场营销等专业的教授，不定期地为这些年轻人讲授实用的前沿知识。

越来越多从中郝峪村走出去的年轻人给赵胜建打电话要求回来加入团队。赵胜建一口答应，但前提是在外工作满三年，“只有在社会泥潭里摸爬滚打一阵子，才能体会人间冷暖，才能有大视野，毕竟创业没那么容易”。

“村里能把年轻人吸引回来，就有前途。”陈焕富感慨。在这位53岁的村干部眼中，这些年轻人是全村最重要的资产。

2013年，这帮年轻人成立了团支部。他们组建的24小时公益救援队伍曾不止一次救出陷入悬崖边的车辆和迷路的游客。

如今的赵胜建仍保持每晚1小时读书和晨起爬山的习惯，“越平缓的路我走得越谨慎，越陡峭的路反而越拼命”。

相比于大学毕业那一年，赵胜建不再孤独，他和他的年轻同伴们正脚踏实地履行当初的承诺：“带着全村人一起向前跑，从不言悔。”

Homecoming: Realization of Chinese Rural Culture

Zhonghaoyu is a small village located deep in the mountains 30 km away from Zibo, Shandong Province. Having blocked the village from the outside world, the mountains have also blocked the village's economic growth for its 360 residents. No one would ever expect the words "shares" or "corporation" to be uttered in this village.

But in fact, great changes have come here, and those responsible were "Alpha Wolf" Zhao Shengjian and his management team — a crew of nine members. These local young people have carved their own unique path of rural development to help their hometown.

The Wisdom of Cooperation and Separation

In 2006, Shengjian graduated from community college and returned home, and was surprised to find himself the only young resident of the village.

He graduated from college as an honor student and the student union president, with a bright future awaiting him. He could join a well-known enterprise or study abroad to pursue a higher degree. But everything changed when he received a letter from home: his father, the Party secretary of the village, had suddenly suffered a serious heart disease and urgently needed care. Being the only child of his family,

Shengjian had no choice but to return home.

At that time, most villagers still relied heavily on agriculture, planting corn and wheat, and lived on a very low income. Shengjian did not want to do this. He did some research, and decided to run a food processing factory pickling balloon flower roots. He led hundreds of local villagers and those from neighboring villages to work hard, and gradually began exporting to South Korea, earning several hundred thousand yuan annually. This gave Shengjian great encouragement and the realization that there was no shortage of opportunities in the countryside. The key was to keep searching and never give up.

Shengjian's factory was on the right track, but an internal crisis which had been lurking in the village for years gradually re-appeared.

Many years earlier in 2003, the village committees had decided to try developing local tourism to boost economic growth. Initially, there were six farmhouses which became tourist spots by providing accommodation, food, and countryside entertainment to visitors. Other villagers caught on, and soon there were 30 such "agri-tainment" farmhouses, all competing with one another by cutting prices. In the end, over half went bankrupt. It seemed that this business model was not suitable for Zhonghaoyu.

Shengjian did some serious market research of such businesses, and spotted the problem. He needed to solve the long-lasting battle which plagued Chinese rural areas: the battle between efficiency and economic growth. Villagers are used to working separately on their farms, which is highly efficient but not very profitable. On the other hand, if the villagers worked together, efficiency would decrease but profits may rise. Shengjian was faced with the puzzle of how to unite the scattered villagers into a group and work together as one collective.

He came up with a bold vision: to form a village "corporation" centered around tourism. The four basic ideas were: (1) unite all the agri-tainment farmhouses of the village to form the corporation and operate collectively; (2) assign a monetary value to lands, housing, and other valuable resources of the village to be used for share subscription; (3) the village committees would serve as the board of directors of the "company" and lead its development; (4) as for dividends, the old, the weak, the sick, and the disabled could enjoy risk-free shares without investment. In addition to such shares, participating villagers could also receive profit-sharing corporate revenue according to the amount of shares they held.

Land quietly entered the market transaction process and was securitized in this bold game. Villagers were able to use their lands to subscribe shares. Each fen (a Chinese land measurement, one fen equals to 66.7 square meters) of land has a value equal to 1,000 yuan, and the value of the villagers' contracted land was evaluated according to the market price. The orchards owned by villagers, such as those with peach trees and chestnut trees, would be evaluated according to diameter. Invested land could be used to plant flowers, seedlings, and grow pick-your-own farms. Also, urban people may "claim" land through the internet, and the villagers would earn money by helping plant on that land.

For Shengjian, it was nothing short than bringing back the dead.

"What is this? Every villager is a shareholder?"

"We don't even have enough money to survive, and you want to start a company?"

Villagers' opposition was strong. How to make villagers willingly surrender their assets and voluntarily buy shares in the new company was a big issue. Even the village committee was concerned.

But Shengjian was stubborn. He drafted a letter of guarantee and pressed his thumbprint on it. "I'll be the first to invest. If it fails, I bear the loss. If it succeeds, I'll share the revenue with everyone." He shouldered immense responsibility for this venture.

After the company was founded, the first task was to attract customers. Shengjian frequently traveled to neighboring cities, carrying bundles of flyers and promotional materials. Though he was rejected many times, slowly people began to learn about the village of Zhonghaoyu.

The remaining 18 agri-tainment farmhouses reluctantly agreed to join the company to give it a try. The corporation collectively managed all 18, set them all at the same price, and also renovated them. "All we need to care about are service quality and sanitary conditions," said Li Xinglan, one of the first 18 shareholders.

A year later, the revenue of all 18 shareholders had doubled. Seeing this, other villagers then joined the company. By 2014, Zhonghaoyu had 90 agri-tainment proprietors.

From "working separately" to "working united", the villagers finally realized that wherever guests came to stay, all the villagers shared the revenue. Everyone began to enjoy the benefits of the cooperation.

Although the villagers were now unified, Shengjian fully encouraged and respected everyone's different characteristics and specialties. Each farmhouse was rated according to different standards of the local tourism department, and according to its unique house specialty. Some had authentic *wowotou* (a traditional Chinese pastry), while others were famous for their particular vegetables, pancakes, or dumplings.

In the past, the per capita annual income of the average Zhonghaoyu villager was less than 2,000 yuan, but that had now risen to more than 45,000 yuan. Risk-free shares rose from 90 yuan per person to more than 4,000. All medical care and insurance for the villagers was provided by the corporation. For three consecutive years, many villagers reinvested their earnings back into the corporation.

Realize the Value of Chinese Rural Culture

Seeing his ideas begin to succeed, Shengjian began to think about how to tailor a unique development path for his hometown. Between the choice of rigidly copying urban industrialization or re-examining Chinese rural culture, Shengjian resolutely chose the latter.

He did not want to use monotonous slogans to decorate the village. Instead, delicate and lively wall murals greet tourists as they enter. All of these murals depict Chinese rural life, such as people gathered around a table making dumplings, and children digging through bird nests in trees — all of which evoke childhood memories. In every few households you see the image of a farm lady holding a plate of special delicacies. The images are rich in color and lifelike. Various restaurants like Auntie's Steamed Buns, Granny's Tofu Shop, and Mr. Liang's Pancake Hut have become village landmarks, tempting tourists to linger.

In Shengjian's opinion, both "hardware" and "software" are indispensable for long-term development in rural tourism, but software provides the purest memories of countryside culture.

"In the past, people never thought about the value of clean air and the nice environment of the countryside, or that homemade specialty dishes could sell at a good price," Zheng Qin said excitedly.

For many tourists, eating in these rural homes brings back childhood memories. A middle-aged tourist once become tearful as he stood in front of a griddle for several hours making pancakes, recalling the memory of his deceased mother who used to make pancakes for him. For younger generations, visiting these farmhouses gives them a chance to interact with nature and agriculture. Students who visit Zhonghaoyu in summer learn how stone mills and stone grinders work while watching them close up and in person.

But an interesting cultural shift has also occurred in Zhonghaoyu over these past successful ten years. The development of the agri-tainment farmhouses has not only helped regenerate the disappearing Chinese rural culture here, but it's also regenerated age-old village rules and folk agreements that had long lost their effectiveness.

As Zhonghaoyu now operates as a corporation, public order has become more highly valued. Common cultural rules such as maintaining a positive and clean village environment have now become an obligation for every villager – or "employee". It is now a company work atmosphere which affects everyone. Village affairs have become corporate affairs.

Village rules and regulations have detailed, strict provisions on littering, raising livestock, and public drunkenness. Once violated, corresponding fines will be deducted from the person's dividends of his/her shares at the end of the year.

The corporation even has rules on upholding filial behavior. According to village regulations, those who are reported as not showing respect to their parents can lose their annual dividends, which will be forwarded to their parents. One case involved an eighty-year-old man who reported to the village committee that his two sons neglected to take care of him for years. At the end of that year, part of the sons' dividends were forwarded to him.

Even Shengjian himself was fined. One night, his friend was drunk and yelled in front of his house. Even though he was the CEO, everyone was equal in the eyes of the regulations. At the end of the year, 100 yuan was deducted from his dividends because of his friend's poor behavior.

"Villagers have been earning more money over the past few years, so now they care more about their reputation," Shengjian said. Over the past two years, there have been few accounts of villagers being fined.

As the positive aspects of Chinese rural culture have been revived, so have some negative aspects been eliminated. For example, every household now has a flush toilet, making these agri-tainment farmhouses more comfortable for urban residents. A few years ago, the village was very dirty, and it was normal to see occasional piles of firewood or dung drying in the sun, which is often a normal scene in northern rural areas. But after years of prosperity, these unpleasant scenes have disappeared. Now, the village roads are clean and orderly, and a charming river gurgles through the village bordered by poplar trees and willows on the bank, creating a pleasant environment.

Every family hangs village regulations on their walls, and they are sincere in keeping these regulations. Shengjian recalled how one day he witnessed a tourist tossing an ice cream wrapper on the ground, and a five-year-old boy immediately ran out to pick it up and throw it into the dustbin.

It is not only the villagers who benefit, but also the village committee. The collective income of the village is now more than 3,000,000 yuan per year, compared to only a few thousand per year in the past. This money means that the committee can invest more money into public affairs, services and utilities.

In order to relieve the worries of elder villagers and reduce the burden on their children, the corporation also built a new retirement home in 2014 with a total of 28 beds. Elderly villagers over 70 years old are free to move in and receive free medical care, and all living expenses are equally borne by the village committee and the company. The company also built a cemetery from a piece of unused land in the village, where villagers can choose to be buried at no charge.

A new sanatorium in the village is still under construction. The idea came from Shengjian, who conceived of it while watching his father lie helplessly in his sickbed. From that time, he dreamed that everyone could one day enjoy better medical services.

Bring the Phoenix Back Home

In the eyes of Chen Huanfu, deputy director of the village committee, the changes in the village over the past decade have been "earth-shattering". But how they'd go forward and how far they could go depended solely on the people.

Shengjian has been troubled by this problem more than once. For more than ten years, he tried to hire professional management people from other cities, but none stayed. After much self-reflection, he then realized: "Those people had no emotional connection to the village. They only cared for their own interests and future." He wondered how to bring back hometown young villagers who had gone to work in other places.

"I'd call them and paint a bright future for them," Shengjian said with a smile. In 2010, after receiving Shengjian's call, Wang Zuo immediately quit his machinery job and went back to the village. "My hometown is developing, and I need to do something to make it better," Wang Zuo recalled.

Over the past several years, Wang Zuo has witnessed the huge transformation of the village and the return of his childhood friends.

Market developers, catering services, design and operations....these young people have all devoted their different talents to the good of their hometown. The village even has its own WeChat social media account, a paintball club, and a team-building camp. Shengjian also thought about making the village roads look more artistic by painting more murals, building tree houses, and arranging flower boxes on street home windowsills which were popular in small European cities.

The return of these young people will undoubtedly bring endless vitality to the village. More than once villagers have come across these young people sitting around discussing future development plans for the village.

Shengjian also invited more than a dozen professors from Beijing and Shandong specializing in tourism management and marketing to teach the inexperienced young people cutting-edge information.

More and more young people who have left the village continued to call Shengjian, asking to come back to the village and join his team. Shengjian agreed, but with the requirement that they should have at least three years working experience outside the village. "Only those who have lived in the quagmire of society for a while can truly appreciate the warmth of a small village and have a bigger vision. You need this broader perspective before trying to manage an enterprise."

"As long as we can attract young people to return, there will be a future for the village," said Chen Huanfu. This 53-year-old village official believes that these young people are the most important assets of the village.

In 2013, Shengjian and his young management team set up a Youth League branch. They also organized a non-profit 24-hour rescue team that has more than once found lost tourists and rescued vehicles trapped on the edge of the nearby cliffs.

These days, Shengjian still keeps the habit of reading for one hour every night and climbing the mountain in the morning. "The smoother the road, the more cautiously I walk. The steeper the road, the harder I try."

Compared to ten years ago when he was the only one to return home, Shengjian is now no longer alone. He and his young companions work hard every day to fulfill their primary goal: "Bring the whole village forward, and don't look back."

“闪修侠”掘金智能硬件维修市场

“Shanxiuxia” & Intelligent Hardware Maintenance Market

作者：王聪聪
翻译：韩芙芸

“闪修侠”掘金智能硬件维修市场

21岁在杭州创办自己的第一家智能手机维修店时，王源觉得那是最幸福的日子，“每天心里都有一团火”。

他4年内开出了5家手机维修连锁店。2015年1月，“几乎每一步都踩准了市场节奏”的王源迎来了O2O商业模式的风口，他果断决定关闭线下店，专做上门维修服务。目前，这家名为“闪修侠”的公司已完成数亿元的5轮融资，投后估值超20亿元。

创业以来，王源见证了智能手机市场的变迁，从苹果一家独大到华为、OPPO、小米等中国品牌崛起赶超。移动互联网时代人们对智能手机的严重依赖，也让手机售后市场蓬勃发展，“保守估计每年需要维修的手机在两亿台以上，加上其他智能硬件维修的需求，市场规模超千亿元”。

时光荏苒，风口变换，上门洗车、上门美甲等一大批O2O公司倒闭了，“闪修侠”

却依然在扩大市场，目前业务覆盖30多个城市，占据手机上门维修市场份额的60%以上。“我们一直在围绕用户需求快速迭代服务，而不是造出伪需求。”王源对记者坦言，在资本大量注入时会“有些膨胀”，面对残酷的市场竞争和巨头进入，只能逼自己快速成长，带领团队直面挑战。

看准机会，自学成为最早修智能手机的人

如果继续攻读大学的专业，王源可能有一份舒适的“码农”工作，但是他从小喜欢拆装，一直对硬件非常感兴趣，“走自己的路，做想做的事”的念头激励着他在2010年初应聘到苹果公司做售后。

当年9月，iPhone4上市，带动了智能手机市场的火爆。王源很快发现，不少人的手机损坏并不在保修范围内，比如摔坏了、进水了，“当时苹果有一个规定是加1700元换一台新手机。我想，怎么能这么贵？自己去做专业维修应该有机会。”

开店要租房子、买设备、招人，王源一

点儿都没觉得琐碎麻烦，从来没有过的体验反而让他感觉“有趣”。启动资金是个大问题，他用光了工作两年的积蓄，刷爆了信用卡，再和父母软磨硬泡，终于凑出十多万元。2011年4月，他在杭州市百脑汇开了一间40平方米的手机售后服务店，“我是浙江最早一批修智能手机的人，每天在国内外论坛泡到深夜，琢磨怎么拆，怎么越狱，怎么刷机。”

第一单生意在开店半个月后终于来了。王源修得满头大汗，对方看着一脸通红的他，问：“哥们儿，怎么样了？”

“不好意思，我修坏了。”王源至今回想起来仍然觉得场面尴尬，“我买了一个新手机给客户，旧手机拿回来继续研究。”就这样半年赔了10万元，他的技术和经验与日俱增。

如今，在距离西湖区灵隐寺和蚂蚁金服公司不远的“闪修侠”CEO办公室里，最显眼的书架上摆放着王源创业之初修坏的各种型号的手机。

“有辛酸泪也有成就感。”这位个子高

大、脸圆圆的90后创始人告诉记者，当时常常想起来吃第一顿饭时已经下午3点，晚上11点在公交车上总能睡着。最惨的是被物业逼着交房租，下午不交就要断电。

因为修得快、修得好，王源很快赚到第一桶金——20万元。2011年年底，王源做了一个大胆的决定——扩店，并且把所有的钱全部投入装修。这是因为他总结后发现，客户看中的一是技术，二是体验。

那间120平方米的办公室，三分之二的面积是客户接待区，备有电视、沙发、茶水，这在当时大部分手机维修店还是小摊位的情况下独树一帜，几乎每天来修手机的客户都能排到电梯口。

3年后，王源在距杭州1小时车程的萧山、绍兴等地开了5家智能手机直营连锁店。

果断关闭盈利的线下店转战上门维修

智能手机不断更新，人们的生活节奏越来越快。2014年下半年，王源发现手机维修市场发生了很大的变化，竞争者涌入这个行业，但水平参差不齐，价格不透明、偷换零部件、维修时间太长等问题困扰着消费者。同时，连锁店异地管理的问题也让他头疼，“修手机是非标品，每个手机的故障不一样，总会出现维修人员接私单的情况”。

“只要发现了问题，就没有什么是我解决不了的。”王源开始深刻思考如何破局，搜索国内外可以借鉴的模式，“还去一家寺庙待了三天，从创业的快节奏中暂停，打坐沉思”。

之所以想到上门维修的点子，是因为一位朋友有一天晚上打电话给他，想让他派人到家里帮自己的母亲修手机，“我出打车费！”这句话仿佛石破天惊，点醒了王源，“上门服务简直是为我们量身定制的凤凰涅槃计划！”

在当时的他看来，选择O2O是天时地利人和：“天时”是指客户对时间的刚性需求兴起，“再早几年上门谁都不信你”；“地利”是国家陆续推出一系列“双创”利好政策，资本热捧O2O；“人和”是自己有线下店技术经验和供应链等资源积累。

"原来一个线下店只能覆盖5公里，现在各地的客户都可以一键预约；原来一年交100万元房租，现在店面成本省了。"王源越想越兴奋，好像"戴着望远镜都看不到天花板"。

他踌躇满志，自己投入100万元，2015年1月6日，"闪修侠"成立。

然而，"心里装着一团火"的王源没想到的是，一场真正的火灾突如其来。2015年4月，由于员工玩儿打火机导致过失失火，他的一家店面全部烧光，还波及百脑汇一层楼的商户。

"有员工受伤进了ICU，公安、消防为了防止老板跑路，要求我不能出杭州。"那是他创业以来面对的最大危机，上百万元的赔偿压力和巨大的精神压力都搁在了25岁的王源身上。度过了难眠之夜后，白天他还要故作镇定，"不能在员工面前表现出没有办法，要不然军心就散了"。

以后每次遇到困难时，王源总会回想起火灾后的境况，"没有什么坎儿是迈不过去的，今天让你非常痛苦的问题，用比较长远的目光去看会发现非常简单。”

当时正在接洽的米仓资本投资人看到熬了通宵，一头乱发的王源，并没有放弃投资，反而鼓励他说：“和过去就此别过，‘闪修侠’肯定能干好。”

一个月后，500万元天使轮融资到账。王源陆续关闭了其他4家尚在盈利的线下店，全心投入上门维修服务的大市场。

“500万噼里啪啦只剩下15万，每天却只有三五单”

资本的助力让王源感到“海阔天空”，也“有些膨胀”。

互联网产业资深从业人士司新颖表示，O2O上门服务解决的是用户便捷性问题，但线下店转型线上绝非易事，获客问题首当其冲，运营又是难上加难，只有专业的市场推广才能践行这种模式。

线下店有固定客源，怎么让消费者信赖

一家线上的创业公司？"当时找客户真的找到怀疑人生，怀疑自己。"王源和团队一开始陷入了O2O靠补贴拉流量的惯性思维里，但效果甚微。

"500万噼里啪啦只剩下15万，每天却只有三五单。"王源对记者说，当时团队忽略了最重要的一环——手机维修低频、偶发，一部手机大多一年只修一两次，哪天坏时间不确定，这决定了"闪修侠"不能用大多数互联网公司拉流量的打法。

2015年年底是"闪修侠"最艰难的一段日子，"眼看要过年了，员工的工资发不出来，供应链的资金也要断"。王源给所有员工开了电话会议，他说："公司出了问题责任在我，如果现在能跟着我，我一定会带领大家走下去！"

王源把车卖了，去银行借了200万元给员工发了工资，还上了供应商的欠款。他带着团队冷静下来，仔细分析发现，只有一个渠道管用——已经修过手机的用户会不断介绍新的用户，这是口碑的力量。闪修侠开始转变策略，把外围推广全部砍掉，静下心来专心做服务，“大概花了两三个月的时间梳理制度、供应链、服务标准、专业技术”。

“技术只是敲门砖，我们努力让技术‘有温度’。”王源说，“闪修侠”首先要求“千人一面”，一千个客户体验到闪修侠的流程是一样的。现在要求“千人千面”，在保证标准流程的基础上，让客户感受到品质服务，在维修工程师的言谈沟通培训上下功夫。现在，“闪修侠”在线报价全国统一，全程视频录像，并且首创了手机上门维修的服务标准，还设立了六重保障全方位保证服务品质。

经历了企业生死考验，如今王源经常说的一句话是，“用户服务是‘闪修侠’的生命之本，一旦在这个层面懈怠就会倒闭！”

几位投资人都是在不经意间体验了“闪修侠”的服务后主动找上门来的，比如同创伟业合伙人东明。有一次，他的手机不慎进水，同事推荐的“闪修侠”工程师不到一小时便处理好故障。后来，他问了一圈发现，办公室几乎一半的人都用过“闪修侠”。

2016年4月，“闪修侠”的现金流“开

始回正"。一个月后，第二笔融资1000万元到账。

"资本很直接，融资快是因为业务模式简单，每一单都赚钱，市场又足够大。"王源信心满满。

一战成名，创业的每一天平凡又闪亮

2018年，中国智能手机市场全年总出货量为3.96亿台，华为（含荣耀）占据27%的市场份额，接下来依次为OPPO、vivo、小米。苹果出货量连续3年下跌，占9%的市场份额。

王源看到使用国产品牌手机的年轻人越来越多，于是他主动开拓市场，与手机品牌厂商进行合作，负责他们的售后维修服务，比如小米、魅族。

"手机一般在使用8个月后开始出现维修需求，18～24个月为维修高峰期。"他介绍，如今"闪修侠"在全国拥有1200多名维修工程师，每个月平均接单15万～20

万单，平均单价400元，艾媒咨询等多方市场数据分析报告表明，“闪修侠”已经成为手机上门维修服务的头部公司。

赢得了客户口碑的“闪修侠”，品牌影响力越来越大。很多人带着梦想加入这家创业公司，有在大公司管理过几千人团队的70后，有从海外学成归来的80后，有在杭州上了大学留下的90后……

“从0到1时想的是如何活下来，现在更多的是想如何让团队和公司一起成长。”90后王源如今长了白发，“一根白发可能就是一个不眠的夜晚或者焦头烂额的事，既是煎熬，也促使我成长”。

他最近翻到当初开一家小店时的进货记录，感到“很燃很幸福”。O2O的风口来了又走，但是“闪修侠”一直活在真实的客户需求里”，每一天都平凡又闪亮，“我永远在路上”。

"Shanxiuxia" & Intelligent Hardware Maintenance Market

When 21-year-old Wang Yuan opened his first smartphone repair store in Hangzhou, he believed it was the happiest day. "Every day, there is a fire burning in my heart."

He opened five mobile phone repair chains in four years. "Almost every step he took was on the market rhythm", Wang Yuan got to know the O2O business model in January 2015. Then he decisively closed offline stores to specialize in door-to-door repair services. At present, the company named Shanxiuxia (Flash Repairman) completed five rounds of hundreds of millions of yuan financing, with a post-money valuation of over two billion yuan.

Since its inception, Wang Yuan has witnessed changes in the smartphone market from Apple's dominance to the rise of Chinese brands such as Huawei, OPPO, and Xiaomi. The heavy reliance on smartphones in the mobile internet era has also enabled the after-sales service market to flourish. "It is conservatively estimated that more than 200 million mobile phones need to be repaired each year, with the addition of the need for other smart hardware repairs, the market size will exceed 100 billion yuan."

As time passed by, businesses got their rise and fall. While many O2O companies such as door-to-door car washes, door-to-door manicures, etc. closed down, Shanxiuxia was still expanding its market. Its current services cover more than 30 cities, accounting for more than 60% of the mobile phone door-to-door repair market share. "We have been in a rapid iteration of services on the users' demand, rather than creating pseudo-demand." Wang Yuan told reporters that he became "a little inflated" with large injections of capital. But in the face of brutal market competition and giants' entering, he had to force himself to grow rapidly and lead his team to face the challenge.

The First Person to Fix a Smartphone

Wang Yuan would become a comfortable computer programmer if he continued to study his college major. However, he had liked disassembling things since childhood and had been very interested in hardware. The thought of "going your own way to do what you want to do" inspired him to apply to work in customer service at Apple Inc. in early 2010.

In September of that year, the iPhone 4 went on sale, driving a boom in the smartphone market. Wang Yuan soon found that many people's mobile phone damage was not covered by the warranty, such as broken or water-soaked. "At that time, Apple had a provision of paying an extra 1700 yuan to exchange for a new phone. I thought to myself, how could it be so expensive? There should be a chance for me to do smartphone repairs myself."

To start a business, you have to rent a place, buy equipment, and hire staff. Wang Yuan did not feel bothered to do all these things; instead, he found them "interesting" as he had never experienced it before. Startup funds were a big problem. He used up all his savings from his two years of work, maxed out his credit card, importuned his parents, and finally collected more than ten thousand yuan. In April 2011, he opened a 40 square-meter smartphone after-sales service store in Buynow Building, Hangzhou. "I am one of the first people in Zhejiang to repair smartphones. Every day I used to soak in the domestic and foreign forums into the night, pondering how to dismantle, how to boot a smartphone."

The first business order finally came half a month after his store opened. Wang Yuan was repairing with excessive sweat on his head, blushing. The client looked at him asked, "Man, how is it?"

"Sorry I've made it worse." Wang Yuan still felt the awkwardness up to now in retrospect," I bought a new cellphone for the client, kept the old one for further study." In this way, he lost 100,000 yuan in half a year, but his technology and experience improved day by day.

Today, in the CEO's office of Shanxiuxia, not far from Lingyin Temple in Xihu District and Ant Financial Services Group, the most prominent bookshelf contains various types of cellphones Wang Yuan had failed to repair at the beginning of his business.

"There are bitter tears and a sense of accomplishment." The tall, round-faced, post-90s generation founder told reporters that at that time, he often had the first meal after 3 pm and would always fall asleep on the bus around 11 pm. "The worst was when the property management collected the rent. If we couldn't pay it on time, our electricity would be cut off in the afternoon."

Because of the fast and good repair, Wang Yuan quickly earned his first barrel of gold—200,000 yuan. At the end of 2011, Wang Yuan made a bold decision to expand his store and put all the money into renovation. This was because he had done research and found that customers tended to value both the experience and technical support he provided.

In the 120 square-meter store, two-thirds was the customer reception area, equipped with TV, sofa, and tea, which was unique when most mobile phone repair stores were small stalls at that time. Therefore almost every day, customers coming to repair phones had to wait in a long queue all the way to the elevator.

Three years later, Wang Yuan opened five chain stores of smartphone repair in Xiaoshan, Shaoxing, and other cities, which are an hour's drive from Hangzhou.

Offline Stores to Door-to-Door

Smartphones are constantly updated, and people's life is getting faster and faster. In the second half of 2014, Wang Yuan found significant changes in the smartphone maintenance market as competitors poured into the industry, but their levels were uneven. Problems bothered consumers concerning untransparent prices, stolen parts, maintenance time being too long, and other issues. At the same time, the chain store management in different places was also a headache for him. "There is no standard for repairing mobile phones, and each phone's faults are different; some maintenance personnel would receive orders in private."

"As long as I find the problem, there's nothing I can't solve." Wang

Yuan began to think deeply about breaking the situation and searching for models at home and abroad that could be used for reference. "I even went to stay in a temple for three days, to pause from the fast pace of entrepreneurship and meditate."

The idea of door-to-door phone repair came to him when a friend called him one night and wanted him to send someone to his house to help repair his mother's cellphone. "I'll pay for the taxi!" It was a eureka moment for Wang Yuan, "Door-to-door service is like a Phoenix Nirvana plan tailored for us!"

In his view, at that time, the choice of O2O was made at the right time, in the right place, and with the right people. The right time referred to the rise of customers' rigid demand for time. "No one would believe you if you proposed such service a few years earlier." The right place referred to a series of favorable policies for entrepreneurship and innovation in China, and the capital was enthusiastic about O2O. The right people referred to Wang's accumulation of resources such as technical experiences and the supply chain of their offline stores.

"Originally, an offline store could only cover a radius of five kilometers. Now customers all over the country can make an appointment with one click. The original cost of a store with a rent of one million yuan a year is saved now." The more Wang Yuan thought about it, the more excited he became as if he "could not see how far the business can go even with a telescope".

He was so ambitious that he invested one million yuan. On January 6, 2015, Shanxiuxia was founded.

However, Wang Yuan, who had "a burning fire in his heart", did not expect a real fire to happen suddenly. In April 2015, one of his stores was burned down due to an employee playing with a lighter, which also affected the stores on the first floor of the Buynow Building.

"There were employees injured and were sent to ICU. The police and fire departments required me not to leave Hangzhou to prevent me from running away." It was the biggest crisis he had faced since he started his business. The pressure of compensation for millions of yuan and tremendous mental pressure weighed on the 25-year-old Wang Yuan. After sleepless nights, he had to pretend to be calm during the day. "I could not show my helplessness in front of the staff; otherwise, the morale will be dispersed."

Whenever he encountered difficulties later in the future, Wang Yuan would always recall his situation after the fire. "There is no obstacle that cannot be overcome. Today's problems that make you suffer will turn out to be very simple in a long-term perspective."

The Ricebank Capital investor who was just in touch saw Wang Yuan, who had stayed up all night with messy hair, and did not give up investing, instead encouraged him, "Say goodbye to the past. Shanxiuxia can certainly do a good job."

A month later, five million yuan of angel round financing was received. Wang Yuan closed four other profitable offline stores and devoted himself to the large market of door-to-door repair services.

Five Million Yuan for 3-5 Orders per Day

The help of capital makes Wang Yuan feel "unrestrained" and

"somewhat inflated".

Internet industrial insider Si Xinying said that the O2O door-to-door service solved the problem of users' convenience, but it was not easy for offline stores to transform online. Customer acquisition was the first to bear the brunt, and operation would be even more difficult. Only with professional marketing could a company practice this model.

Offline stores had stable customers; how to win consumers' trust as an online startup company? "At the time, it makes us doubtful in life and ourselves when it comes to looking for customers." In the beginning, Wang Yuan and his team fell into the inertial thinking of O2O relying on subsidies to pull online traffic, but there was little effect.

"Soon only 150 thousand out of the five million left, but we got only three to five orders a day." Wang Yuan told the reporters that his team overlooked the most important point: mobile phone maintenance is low-frequent and occasional. A mobile phone is repaired once or twice a year at most and it is uncertain it will develop a fault, which determines that Shanxiuxia cannot use the method as most internet companies to pull traffic.

The end of 2015 is the most challenging period for Shanxiuxia. "The Lunar New Year was coming. Employees are not paid, and the funds in the supply chain were going to be cut off." Wang Yuan held a teleconference with all employees. He said, "I claim the responsibility for the problem of the company. If you still choose to work with me, I will continue leading the team."

Wang Yuan sold his car and loaned two million yuan from the

bank to pay the staff and the suppliers. He calmed down with his team, analyzed carefully, and found that only one channel worked: Customers who had their cell phones repaired here would introduce new customers, which was the power of word of mouth. Shanxiuxia began to change its strategy, cut down all the peripheral promotion, and concentrate on service. "It took about two or three months to sort out the system, supply chain, service standards, and technology".

"Technology is just a stepping stone. We endeavor to make the technology 'warm'." Wang Yuan said that Shanxiuxia used to require "one unified service for a thousand people", meaning 1,000 customers would experience the same process from Shanxiuxia. Now it required "a thousand ways for a thousand people", meaning that on the basis of the standard process, they would try to make the customers feel quality service after they trained the maintenance engineers on their language communication skills. Now, Shanxiuxia online quotes unified prices throughout the country, provides video recording of its whole process, firstly establishes cell phone door-to-door maintenance service standards and a six-fold guarantee to ensure all-round service quality.

Having experienced the life and death of an enterprise, Wang Yuan often said now, "Serving the users' service is the lifeline of Shanxiuxia. Once we slack at this, we will go bankrupt!"

Several investors aproached them and offered to invest in Shanxiuxia after having inadvertently experienced its service, including Ming Dong, a partner of Cowin Capital. On one occasion, his cell phone was accidentally soaked, and the engineer from Shanxiuxia, recommended by his colleagues, fixed the problem in less than an hour. Later, he asked around and found that almost half of the staff had ever used Shanxiuxia.

In April 2016, Shanxiuxia's cash flow "get back to positive". A month later, the second financing of ten million yuan was received.

"Capital is direct. The financing is fast because our business model is simple. Every order makes money, and the market is big enough." Wang Yuan was full of confidence.

Make a Name

In 2018, China's smartphone shipments reached 396 million units, with Huawei (including Honor) accounting for 27% of the volumes, followed by OPPO, Vivo, and Xiaomi. Apple's shipments had declined for three consecutive years, accounting for 9% of the market.

When Wang Yuan found that more and more young people were beginning to use domestic brands, he took the initiative to explore the market and cooperate with smartphone manufacturers such as Xiaomi and Meizu on taking over their after-sales maintenance services.

"A smartphone may need to be repaired in eight months of use, and the peak period is 18-24 months." He introduced that now Shanxiuxia had more than 1,200 maintenance engineers, handling an average of 150-200 thousand orders per month, and the average price was 400 yuan per order. According to the market data analysis report of iiMedia Research and other companies, Shanxiuxia had become the leading company in smartphone repair service.

Having won the best reputation among their clients, Shanxiuxia's brand influence was growing. Many people joined it with their dreams, including the post-70s who once managed a team of several thousand people in large companies, the post-80s who returned from overseas studies, and the post-90s who recently graduated from universities in Hangzhou.

"From 0 to 1, I was thinking about how to survive. Now I am thinking more about how to make the team and my company grow together." Wang Yuan, a post-90s, now grew gray hair. "A gray hair may be caused by a sleepless night or a troublesome problem, which is not only suffering but also prompting me to grow up."

Recently, he happened to turn to the purchase records of the small store he first opened and felt "very exhilarated and happy". The wind of O2O had come and gone, but Shanxiuxia "has been living in the real needs of clients". Every day is ordinary and shining. "I will always be on the road."

地学博士做地质公园科普年入超 2000 万元

Doctor of Geoscience Promoting Popular Science in Geoparks

作者：胡　林　雷　宇
翻译：韩芙芸

地学博士做地质公园科普年入超 2000 万元

打开App“脚爬客”，搜索地学博士李鑫的“脚印”，几乎每次都是在各大世界级或者国家级的地质公园里与众多科普志愿者一起探索地学的奥秘，足迹覆盖大江南北。

这个由李鑫创立的国内首家专注于地学科普自然体验的网络社区里，汇集了数万名地学科普、自然教育的爱好者，还有数以千计的专业科普志愿者。仅2018年一年，他们就开展了数百场地质公园科普活动。

一次畅谈吸引了多位地质公园负责人

“地球太奇妙了，太多的地理科学等着我们去研究、体验和分享。”打小就迷恋大自然的李鑫喜欢登山、徒步、游泳，甚至每两年就会喜欢上一个新的户外运动，“为的就是从不同的领域去研究大自然”。

在中国地质大学（武汉）读本科和研究生时，李鑫选的都是地质工程方向。研二那年，他甚至跑到了内蒙古自治区阿拉善盟额济纳旗，在西北大漠里待了整整一年，去戈壁滩采样做实验，研究黑河古河道调水后的生态治理。

2011 年，李鑫辞职回到母校攻读环境地质方向的博士。他所在的课题组开始涉足地质遗迹保护开发和地质公园领域，他也多次奔赴广西、山西、福建等地，参与了当地地质公园项目的申报、规划和建设。

地质公园最初由欧洲发起，旨在促进地球生态、地质保育及人类生存发展。在北京召开的第一次世界地质公园年会上，李鑫发现，国外的地质公园建设不仅与自然环境结合紧密，更要求开展一系列科普活动，让每一个当地人都了解地质公园，推动全民科普。

结合项目经历和个人研究，李鑫在一次全国地质公园工作交流会上畅谈自己的思考，没想到，一下子吸引了好几位地质公园管理负责人前来“取经”。

“地质公园在国内发展时间不长，很多方面缺乏指导，他们不了解如何建设、怎样升级。”为了给予对方细致、专业的解答，李鑫搜集资料并结合项目经验，带领课题组分门别类整理出了100多个文件夹，免费提供给了有需求的地质公园负责人。

随着交流的深入，大家发现一对一的邮件交流效率太低，信息更新也慢。李鑫产生了一个新想法：何不建立一个网站，将资料和信息及时上传更新，为地质公园管理负责人搭建行业交流平台，让他们能够快速下载使用？

说干就干，一个面向全国的地质（矿山）公园免费提供技术支持、行业资讯、地学科普、公园宣传推广的公益性网络平台搭建起来，取名为“地质公园之家”，并通过微博、微信等新媒体手段向公众推介。

将研究课题升级为创业项目

李鑫和“地质公园之家”良好的口碑很快被行业所熟知。

地质公园的申报建设需要有科研论文、调查数据、对比研究等地质科学研究支撑，涵盖地质、生物、人文等多个领域。和国外相比，国内的地质公园建设差距较大。

国外的地质公园有哪些经验可以借鉴？中国的地质公园发展方向在哪里，如何因地制宜？李鑫开始从产业的视角去思考中国地质公园的未来。

彼时正逢湖北省出台相关政策，鼓励在职科研人员、高校的博士生创业，李鑫决定将研究课题升级为创业项目。

他拉上一位同学合伙，成立武汉地学之旅信息技术有限公司，并注册“地质公园之家”商标。他还根据“地质公园”英语单词Geoparker的音译，提出“脚爬客”这一理念，倡导爱护地球、推动地质保育。

为了搜集“地质公园之家”的各类资料，李鑫去加拿大、澳大利亚、中国香港等地参加学术会议时，特意观察当地的地质公园科普模式。

考察香港世界地质公园时，李鑫待了两个多月。他看到，即使修一条路，当地也会做详细周密的规划、论证，尽可能保护原貌，减少对大自然的侵扰。

此外，香港世界地质公园的资料会以视频、PPT等信息化方式呈现出来，公众能免费下载学习。公园还配备了经过科学培训的“自然导赏员”，定期开设“常规导赏活动”，“地学科普做得特别细致，从小学生到大学生，都能讲一些地学知识，很震撼”。

对比之下，李鑫意识到，国内的地质公园科普推广大有可为。

恰巧在当年，广东省丹霞山世界地质公园管委会的负责人主动找上李鑫，想请他帮忙招募一批地学科普志愿者。以前，丹霞山世界地质公园招募的志愿者大都局限于本省，并且非地学专业，地学科普推广的难题一直困扰着他们。

李鑫通过“地质公园之家”等多个渠道发布了招募信息，一下子收到来自北京大学、武汉大学、中国地质大学等全国知名高校的300多张报名表，涵盖地质（构造、矿物、古生物、化石、天体）、植物、昆虫、动物、鸟类、鱼类、户外运动、传媒、影像等多个专业和职业的地学旅游爱好者。

这一结果震撼了丹霞山世界地质公园管委会的负责人。双方一拍即合，选出 30 名科普志愿者，联合举办了“2014 丹霞山科普志愿者训练营”活动。

科普志愿者发挥各自的专业优势，给山川河流摸底画像，分析生物多样性，调查人文历史，根据考察记录绘制研学旅游线路，形成了详细的科普报告。

大家还利用新浪、搜狐、知乎等网络媒体传播科普日记，吸引游客前往观察体验，这一创新受到丹霞山世界地质公园管委会的高度赞赏，也让李鑫的团队收获了项目的“第一桶金”。

2015 年 7 月，丹霞山再度与“脚爬客”联手。

在第二期丹霞山科普志愿者训练营中，李鑫结合往期的经验调整实训任务，有地质遗迹、生物多样性科普讲座，实地考察科考线路，植物标本采集，绘制丹霞地貌演变图、丹霞岩层剖析图等，增加志愿者的地质科普知识和体验。

“沉积岩是地球的‘日记本’、云南石林是拔地而起的‘黑森林’、丹霞地貌是大自然的印象派画作……”李鑫说，科普就是要用通俗易懂的方式，将当地的自然、人文、历史讲述成一个个生动的科普故事，要接地气。

2017年，“脚爬客”携手国家地质公园网络中心主办的“首届最美地球印记”国家地质公园摄影大赛，获得百万人次关注。

作为国内首个地学科普App，“脚爬客”涵盖地质公园智能导览、地质公园脚印、地质公园游记等功能，为自然保护地提供申报规划、建设咨询以及训练营、校园行、科普云等科普服务。

他告诉记者，目前，他们先后与200多家地质公园达成战略合作，在重庆、广东、山东、甘肃等省打造出500多条地质科普旅游线路。

除了给自然资源保护地提供传统的咨询申报服务，李鑫团队充分利用“地质专业知识+互联网”，在活动中挖掘当地的科普价值。“比如，当地从地质公园申报到科普形象宣传、志愿者招募、公园科普解说、科普信息化，每年都会有更新的需求”。

围绕地质公园申报咨询、科普训练营、科普教育等几大业务板块，2018 年“脚爬客”平台年营收近 2400 万元。

此外，团队承担了 30 余项自然保护地申报规划建设服务和百余项自然保护地线上线下科普服务，招募了 25880 名地学科普志愿者，举办了 118 场地质公园科普校园行讲座，与全国 102 所高校建立了合作。

李鑫举例，团队先后组织专家及志愿者，仅在丹霞山世界地质公园就开展了 10 多次科普，帮当地开发出 20 多条地质科普游玩路线。

连续三次参与创业　总结出“创之道”

成功的背后没有太多偶然。创立“脚爬客”之前，李鑫有过多次创业经历。

2006 年，李鑫参与了一个升学的教育项目，老板看中了他的业务开拓能力，一次性给出 30 万元，让他去北京创立分公司。

半年时间，李鑫拿下河北、内蒙古等北方5省的市场。可不久，因为觉得行业和所学专业相差较大，他选择离开。

2007年，他加入地大一家做非金属矿物加工的产学研企业。两年多里，由于公司的技术专家侧重于科研，对产品质量没有严格把关，企业失去市场，经营不善，导致巨额亏损。李鑫被迫辞职。

2009年，一家做浅层低温能开发的校友企业力邀李鑫加盟，可这个产学研项目融资需求太大，后续投资无法跟进，经营不下去，他只得退出。

“创业就是找对人、说对话、干对事”，连续三次参与创业，李鑫如是总结自己的“创之道”。

“带头去跑市场，是初创期创始人的首要任务，一定要坚持。只有业务上的‘攻城拔寨’，才能给团队带来信心。”

“初创期对产品质量把关尤为重要，要在行业内打造出自己的产品标准，在垂直领域细分市场做到第一才有机会。”这位地学博士说。

Doctor of Geoscience Promoting Popular Science in Geoparks

Open the App "Geoparker" and search for the "footprints" of Dr. Li Xin, a geoscientist. You will most likely find that he is exploring the mysteries of geoscience with many popular science volunteers in world-class or national geoparks all over the country.

Founded by Li Xin, this first online community in China focuses on the natural experience of geoscience popularization, bringing together tens of thousands of enthusiasts on geoscience popularization and natural education, as well as thousands of professional volunteers. In 2018 alone, they carried out hundreds of popular science activities in geoparks.

A Talk Attracts the Attention of Geopark Managers

"The earth is marvelous, and there are so many geosciences waiting for us to study, experience, and share." Li Xin, who has been fascinated with nature since childhood, likes mountain climbing, hiking, swimming, and even enjoys a new outdoor sport every two years, "to study nature from different fields".

When he was an undergraduate and graduate student at China University of Geosciences (Wuhan), Li Xin chose the same major of geological engineering. In his second year of graduate school, he even went to Ejin Banner, Alaxa League in Inner Mongolia Autonomous Region. He stayed in the desert there for a whole year to sample and do experiments in the Gobi Desert and studied the ecological management of the ancient Heihe River after water diversion.

In 2011, Li Xin resigned and returned to his alma mater to study for a doctorate in environmental geology. The research team he joined began to set foot in geological heritage protection and developing geoparks. He also went to Guangxi, Shanxi, Fujian, and other places to participate in the application, planning, and construction of local Geopark projects.

Europe originally initiated geoparks to promote the earth's ecology, geological conservation, and human survival and development. At the first annual meeting of the World Geoparks held in Beijing, Li Xin found that the construction of foreign geoparks is not only closely integrated with the natural environment but also provides a series of popular science activities to make every local know about geoparks and promote the popularization of science among the general public.

Combining his project experience and personal research, Li Xin talked about his thoughts at a national geopark exchange meeting. Unexpectedly, he attracted several geopark managers to come to "learn from his experience".

"Geoparks are relatively new in China, and the managers lack experience in many aspects like how to build and upgrade them." Li Xin collected information, combined with his own project experience, and sorted out more than 100 folders in different categories to give detailed and professional answers. His research team provided them to the Geopark managers in need free of charge.

With further communication, people found that one-to-one email communication was inefficient and information updates were slow. Li Xin came up with a new idea: Why not set up a website to upload and update data and information in time, and build an industry communication platform for Geopark managers?

No sooner said than done. A public welfare network platform countrywide had been set up to provide free technical support, industry information, geoscience popularization, and park promotion for geoparks and was named "Home of Geoparks". It was introduced to the public through new media such as Weibo and WeChat.

From Research Projects to Entrepreneurial Projects

The excellent reputation of Li Xin and his "Home of Geoparks" soon became known in the industry.

The application and construction of geoparks need to be supported by scientific research such as scientific research papers, survey data, and comparative research, involving various fields like geology, biology and humanities. Compared with other countries, the geoparks in China were far less developed.

What experiences can be learned from the geoparks abroad? What is the direction of China's geoparks? How do they adapt to local conditions? Li Xin began to think about the future of China's geoparks from an industrial perspective.

Right on occasion, Hubei Province issued relevant policies to encourage in-service scientific research personnel, university doctoral students to start their own businesses. Li Xin decided to upgrade his research topic to an entrepreneurial project.

He got a classmate into a partnership to set up Wuhan Geoscience Journey Information Technology Co., Ltd. and registered the trademark for Home of Geoparks. Based on the English word for geoparks, he also put forward the concept of "geoparker" to advocate the love for the earth and promote geological conservation.

To collect all kinds of information for "Home of Geoparks", Li Xin specially observed their local geopark science activities when he attended academic conferences in Canada, Australia, China's Hong Kong, and other places.

During a visit to the Hong Kong UNESCO Global Geopark, Li Xin stayed for more than two months. He found that even if before a road was built, they would make detailed planning and demonstration, as far as possible to protect the original appearance, reduce the intrusion to nature.

Furthermore, the Hong Kong UNESCO Global Geopark information is presented by video, PowerPoint slides, and other digital forms so that the public can download it for free. The park also has science-trained "nature guides", who regularly hold "routine guide activities". "They did a particularly meticulous work on geology science education. Students from primary school to college can talk about some geoscience knowledge. It's very impressive."

In contrast, Li Xin realized that there was great potential for geopark popular science on China's mainland.

Coincidentally in that year, the chairperson of the Danxiashan Global Geopark Management Committee, Guangdong Province, approached Li Xin and asked him to help recruit a group of geoscience volunteers. Before, Danxiashan Global Geopark recruited volunteers mainly in its province and many were not majoring in geoscience. The problem of promoting had been bothering them.

Li Xin released recruitment information through the "Home of Geoparks" and other channels, and all at once received more than 300 applications from Peking University, Wuhan University, China University of Geosciences, and other well-known universities in the country, including geoscience enthusiasts and those majoring in geology (tectonics, minerals, paleontology, fossils, celestial bodies), plants, insects, animals, birds, fish, outdoor sports, media, video, etc.

The result impressed the chairperson of the Danxiashan Global Geopark Management Committee. The two sides worked together to select 30 popular science volunteers and jointly organized "2014 Mount Danxia Volunteer Training Camp".

These volunteers drew on their expertise to draw maps for mountains and rivers, analyze biodiversity, investigate humanity history, design research and tourist routes according to exploration records, and finally formed a detailed science report.

They also used Sina, Sohu, Zhihu, and other online media to publish science diaries and attract tourists to go to observe and experience. The innovation was highly appreciated by the Danxiashan Global Geopark

Management Committee, which also brought Li Xin's team "the first bucket of gold."

In July 2015, Danxiashan organized the event again jointly with Geoparker.

In the second volunteer training camp, Li Xin adjusted the training program from the previous experience to include science lectures on geological relics and biodiversity, field visits to science expedition routes, plant specimen collection, mapping Danxia landform geomorphological evolution map, Danxia rock formation profile chart, etc. to increase the volunteers' knowledge and experience of geosciences.

"Sedimentary rock is the earth's 'diary'. Yunnan's Stone Forest is a 'black forest' rising straight from the ground. Danxia landform is nature's impressionist painting..." Li Xin said that popular science should use an easy-to-understand way to turn the local natural and human history into vivid science stories.

In 2017, Geoparker cohosted the "First Most Beautiful Earth Imprint" National Geopark Photography Competition with the National Geopark Network Center and attracted millions of followers.

Geoparker covers the geological park intelligent guide, geological park footprints, geological park travelogue, and other functions as the first domestic geoscience popularization app. It also provides application planning and construction consulting for natural conservation sites and services like training camps, campus activities, and cloud popular science.

He told reporters that at present, they were in strategic cooperation with more than 200 geoparks and designed more than 500 geology science tour routes in Chongqing Municipality, Guangdong, Shandong, Gansu, and other provinces.

Apart from providing traditional consulting and application services to natural resource conservation sites, Li Xin's team makes full use of "geological expertise plus the internet" to develop popular science programs according to local conditions during the cooperation. "For example, every year there will be new demand, such as applications of aspiring geoparks, popular science publicity, volunteer recruitment, park's popular science commentary, digitalization of popular science."

Centering on the geopark application and consulting, popular science training camp, science education as its major business sectors, in 2018, the annual revenue of the Geoparker platform reached 24 million yuan.

Besides, the team undertook more than 30 natural conservation sites' application, planning, and construction services and more than 100 natural conservation sites' online and offline science services, recruited 25,880 geoscience volunteers, held 118 campus lectures on geopark science, and established cooperation with 102 universities nationwide.

Li Xin gave an example that his team had organized more than ten popular science activities led by experts and volunteers in Danxiashan Global Geopark alone and helped the locals develop more than 20 geoscience tour routes.

Three Startups Summed up to a "Way to Success"

There are not too many random factors behind the success. Before founding the Geoparker, Li Xin had many entrepreneurial experiences.

In 2006, Li Xin participated in an education project. The boss believed in his business development ability and gave him 300,000 yuan to set up a Beijing branch. Half a year later, Li Xin won the market of five northern provinces and regions like Hebei, Inner Mongolia, and others. Before long, as he felt there was a big difference between the industry and his major, he chose to leave.

In 2007, he joined a non-metallic mineral processing company under the China University of Geosciences. For more than two years, the company's technical experts mainly focused on scientific research. They did not strictly control its product quality, which caused it to lose the market, resulting in huge losses. Li Xin had to resign.

In 2009, an alumnus' enterprise on shallow low-temperature energy development invited Li Xin to join. But financing needs of this industry-university-research project were too big, follow-up investment was not available, so its business could not go on, he had to quit.

"Entrepreneurship is to find the right person, speak the right words, and do the right thing." Having participated in entrepreneurship three times in a row, Li Xin was summing up his own "way to success".

"Taking the lead in marketing is a top priority for startup founders, and you have to stick to it. Only 'winning the market' can bring confidence to your team.

"Startups should pay particular attention to its product quality. They should create a product standard within the industry and will only succeed when becoming the number one in the vertical market segment," the geoscientist doctor said.

奋斗，一片纸尿裤承载实业强国梦

A Diaper Company Becoming an Industry Power House

作者：谢宛霏　陈燕南
翻译：范逊敏

奋斗，一片纸尿裤承载实业强国梦

“要相信奋斗的力量！”在2018年年初举办的北京大学青年CEO俱乐部的年会上，首届理事长王胜地对在场的全国各地赶来的北大优秀80后、90后创业校友说。

2000年，王胜地从国家级贫困县河南郸城考入北大化学系。他一直怀揣“创造一个世界500强的中国日化企业”的梦想。几次创业失败后，2014年，他再次出发，创办“北京爸爸的选择科技有限公司”。

如今，这家公司不仅在日本建立了研发中心，还在山东临邑建成了亚洲最大的纸尿裤单体生产基地，改变了很多年轻妈妈海淘纸尿裤的现状。王胜地也在一步步实现着他心中实业强国的梦想。

要证明制造业能赚钱

“我想通过奋斗证明中国制造业能赚到

钱。”王胜地说：“以国内现有的技术水平和产业链，完全可以研发生产一款世界最高水准的纸尿裤。只是之前中国没有足够大的品牌去提供高性价比的服务，我们希望改变消费者对国产品牌的认识。”

从北大化学系本科毕业后，王胜地做过科研，也做过进出口贸易，后来赴美国康奈尔大学求学。国人追崇外国生产的纸尿裤让王胜地觉得丢人又无奈，“又不是什么特别高科技的产品”，完全没有必要在国外买，更何况那些纸尿裤质量未必好，让婴儿红屁股等现象时有发生。创业梦想被点燃了，王胜地和清华大学毕业的两位朋友一拍即合，决定研发一款专为中国宝宝设计的既安全又舒适的纸尿裤。

创业之初，王胜地就将“爸爸的选择”定义为“全球化的怪兽”，成为冲破洋品牌价格体系的国产品牌纸尿裤。他非常看好新时代下的中国制造业，“中国的供应链比较齐全、灵活，一些配方改进在美国需要一两年时间，中国一两个月就可以完成。”

在创造出可以和进口纸尿裤媲美的产品

后，他开始下大力气去开拓市场。他把团队分成两拨，一个城市一个城市地去跑展会。

大区销售经理辛星说，王胜地每次在展会上都像打了“鸡血”，他大声吆喝着吸引人流，亲手做尿不湿吸水试验去打动客户，甚至来不及喝上一口水，一天下来都说不出来话了，“每次我们都是整个展会最后一个撤展的”。

王胜地一年跑了100多个展会，几乎每两三天就要换一个城市，场场亲自站台。为了节省时间和成本，他总是选择夕发朝至的火车，每天工作十几个小时，“那段时间好像就不知道累，整个人一直处于兴奋状态”。

他的奋斗精神也感染了团队，辛星说：“为了把品牌推出去，大家都拼尽了全力。”一次在上海参展时，王胜地由于过度疲劳导致心脏供血不足，被送上了急救车。第二天输完液，他又出现在了展会上。

“爸爸的选择”慢慢打开了市场。王胜地认为，随着移动互联网快速发展，产品信息越来越透明，理性的消费者越来越多，“判断产品好坏的标准不在品牌商，而在消费者”。

目前，“爸爸的选择”纸尿裤销售额突破3亿元，被越来越多的年轻妈妈买给孩子使用，全国近一万家母婴店都有该产品，在天猫和京东也开了旗舰店。前不久，“爸爸的选择”纸尿裤在美国开始试销。

“一个国产日化品牌从别人不信到愿意尝试到被认同”，王胜地感到自己被巨大的幸福淹没了。

做公益让创业更快乐

不少创业者在成功后都换了车、换了房，可王胜地还开着三年前刚创业时的那辆车，时不时被员工“霸占”当成拉货车，他自己也依然租住在北京五环外。除了扩大生产、投入研发，他把赚的大部分钱投到了公益事业上。

王胜地出生在河南郸城，那是一个国家级贫困县。他的高中同学韩冰告诉记者，王胜地少年时种过地，“太苦了”，也正是种地这段经历让他发奋考上了北大。他深知读书对孩子，尤其是农村孩子的重要性，有了一些能力后，他一直致力于捐建留守儿童图书馆。

“希望他们可以像我一样通过知识、通过奋斗改变命运。”王胜地说。

韩冰很欣赏王胜地，“他是个特别有情怀的人，能用自己的力量去影响别人”。这也是韩冰愿意从宝洁公司离职和他一起奋斗的原因。

他曾和王胜地一起去乡镇走访，“看到一些五六岁的留守儿童在抽烟，我们都特别痛心”。回京之后，王胜地组织了一些名校大学生利用假期在甘肃、河南的农村进行试点调研，决定将留守儿童图书馆项目推行下去。

王胜地坦言，做这件事最大的问题不是钱，而是长期的维护。如果只是建立一个图书馆，没有人长期管理、没有和孩子们的互动就不会长久，孩子的成长需要引导。

由于公司生产纸尿裤，王胜地还长期给“小水滴”“恒爱之家”等慈善机构捐赠纸尿裤。2016年年初，得知北京“太阳村”慈善机构的孩子需要纸尿裤，王胜地出差结束后连夜赶回北京，安排员工第一时间把纸尿裤准备出来送过去。

看到孩子们可爱的笑脸，王胜地感到很幸福，随后他开始了“雏鸟计划”——一项旨在帮扶社会残障孤弃婴幼儿的慈善公益行动，“以爱之名，放飞每一个希望”。

“每次去慈善机构都要拉一大卡车纸尿裤，王总只要在公司都会和我们一起搬运。他真心想为孩子们做点儿实事，将不少时间和精力都投在了公益上。”公司运营人员穆胜强说。

“我们在做国产新品牌，首先得有好的产品和使命感。做公益可以让创业成为一件快乐的事。”王胜地说。

近50%的经费用于研发

虽然已经熬过了创业瓶颈期，但王胜地依然保持着“鸡血”状态。每天早上一到公司，他先是询问销售部情况，再去研发部跟踪研究进度，然后到会议室跟供应商谈判，走路都带风。其间还要不停地回复4个手机的信息。为了直接倾听消费者的声音，改进、调整产品，王胜地将自己的手机号码留在“爸爸的选择”微信公众号上，担任起了“首席客服”。

有一幕让员工穆胜强难忘，王胜地曾经处理了200万元的不合格品，销毁了大概有几卡车的产品。对产品质量要求精益求精，但王胜地对待自己却截然相反，“这两年没看到他穿过什么新衣服”。因为瘦了15公斤，王胜地原来的呢子大衣肩膀部位肥出了两寸，穿在身上就像个袋子，腰带也长了一大截，支出来甩在身后，“真不像海归！”

“爸爸的选择”公司近50%的经费都花在了研发上。在公司的实验室里，有美国、日本销量最好的纸尿裤的样品。王胜地带着研发人员不断进行比对，找到最好的材料供应商，用人工尿反复测试，力求达到最干爽舒适的吸收效果。一片小小的纸尿裤，“爸爸的选择”研发出了9个专利。

让王胜地最自豪的是公司拉动了就业。

他算过一笔账，如今，“爸爸的选择”在近1万家门店中销售，每家门店配备两三个销售人员，相当于拉动了超过2万人就业。

“创业者要有改变行业的信心，同时要不断创新，为社会创造价值。”在北大青年CEO俱乐部的年会上，王胜地和一些来“取经”的师弟、师妹分享得最多的是“奋斗不已，青春无悔”。

A Diaper Company Becoming an Industry Power House

"Believe in the power of struggle!" said Wang Shengdi at the annual meeting of the Peking University Young CEOs Club held in the beginning of 2018. He is the first president of club, and he spoke these words to the outstanding entrepreneurial alumni of Peking University who came from all over the country to attend the meeting.

In 2000, Wang Shengdi came from Dancheng, a state-level poverty-stricken county in Henan Province to begin his studies at Peking University's Department of Chemistry. After graduating from Peking University with a bachelor's degree in chemistry, Wang worked in scientific research and also in import and export before going to Cornell University in the United States. He had always had the dream to create a Fortune 500 Chinese chemical company. After returning to China and several failed ventures, he set out again in 2014 to found Beijing Daddy's Choice Technology Co., Ltd.

Today, the company not only has a research and development center in Japan, but it also boasts Asia's largest production base for monomers, the millions of molecules which make up the super-absorbent polymers in diapers. The factory is in Linyi, Shandong Province, and this China factory means that many young mothers no longer have to buy overseas diapers anymore. This has helped Wang gradually realize his dream of making the country strong with industry.

Manufacturing Can Be Profitable

"Through our hard work, I want to prove that my country's manufacturing industry can make money," he said. With China's existing technology and industrial infrastructure, it is definitely possible to develop and produce a world-class diaper. "It's just that China did not have a well-known brand before to provide a cost-effective product. We hope to change how consumers understand domestic brands."

He had seen how Chinese consumers rejected domestic brand diapers, and preferred to buy high-priced imported brand diapers from overseas. "It's not a particularly high-tech product," he said. "There is no need to buy diapers from abroad, not to mention that the diapers may be of average quality, which may sometimes cause irritation on the skin of babies." His dream of starting his own business was set alight, so he and two friends who had graduated from Tsinghua University decided to produce a safe and comfortable diaper for the Chinese market.

At the beginning of his business, Wang wanted to define the "Daddy's Choice" brand as "a global monster" which would be a domestic brand diaper that would break through the price system of foreign brands. He is very optimistic about China's manufacturing industry in the new era. "China's supply chain is relatively complete and flexible. Some formula improvements in the United States need one or two years to be completed, while in China it can be made in one or two months."

After producing the diapers that could compete with overseas brands, he made great efforts to open up the market. He divided his team into two groups, and then attended all the trade exhibitions, city by city.

Xin Xing, the regional sales manager of the company, recalled that "During the exhibitions, Wang Shengdi worked with zeal, shouting loudly to attract people, and doing on-the-spot demonstrations to show how the diapers absorbed water to impress the customers. He was talking so much that he didn't even have time to drink water, and by the end of the day his voice was shot. We were always the last company to pack up and leave the exhibition."

Wang attended more than 100 exhibitions in one year to promote his product, which meant traveling to the next city almost every two or three days. In order to save time and expense, he always chose the overnight train and worked more than ten hours a day. "During that time, I didn't feel tired and I was always in a state of excitement."

His tireless efforts also inspired the team. "We all did our best to promote our product and brand," Xin Xing said. During an exhibition once in Shanghai, Wang was actually sent to the hospital in an ambulance due to exhaustion and an insufficient blood supply to his heart. The next day, after a transfusion, he was back at the exhibition.

Slowly, the Daddy's Choice brand was introduced into the market. Wang believes that with the rapid development of the mobile internet, product information is becoming more transparent, and there are more and more rational consumers. "The standards to judge the quality of a product don't depend on the brand, but the consumer."

Currently, sales of "Daddy's Choice" diapers has exceeded 300 million yuan, and more and more mothers are buying them for their children.

They're sold in nearly 10,000 mother and baby stores across the country, and flagship stores have also been opened on online platforms like Tmall and JD.com. Not long ago, Daddy's Choice diapers went on trial sale in the United States.

"A once-unknown domestic brand is now widely known." Wang Shengdi now felt overwhelmed with great happiness.

Public Welfare Makes Entrepreneurship More Rewarding

Many entrepreneurs have upgraded to better cars and bigger houses after their success. Wang still drove the same van he had when he started his business three years ago, which is still sometimes used by employees to pick up goods. He still rent an apartment outside Beijing's fifth ring road. In addition to expanding production and investing in research and development, he has put most of his profit into public welfare undertakings.

Wang was born in Dancheng, a state-level poverty-stricken county. Han Bing, one of his high school classmates, told reporters that Wang had worked on a farm when he was a teenager, and that "Those were difficult days." It was this rough experience that helped him get into Peking University. He knows how important education is for children, especially children in rural areas. He has been committed to donating money to construct libraries for left-behind children, children who stay in the rural areas while their parents work in the cities.

"I hope they can change their life by getting a good education and working hard like I did," Wang Shengdi said.

Han Bing admired Wang very much."He is a passionate, charismatic person." That's why Han Bing was willing to leave his job at Proctor and Gamble to work with him.

They once visited some villages and towns together. "We saw some left-behind children smoking, and we all felt very sad." After returning to Beijing, Wang organized some college students from elite universities to conduct pilot surveys in the rural areas of Gansu and Henan provinces during their vacations, and decided to carry out the left-behind children's library project.

"The biggest problem is not money, but long-term maintenance," Wang said frankly. "If you just build a library but don't consider long-term management and interaction with the children then it won't last long. Children need guidance."

For a long time, the company has also donated diapers to charities such as "Little Water Drop" and "Heng Ai Home". At the beginning of 2016, he learned that children from Beijing's "Sun Village" charity needed diapers. Wang returned to Beijing overnight after his business trip and arranged the staff to send the diapers immediately.

Seeing the lovely smiles on the children's faces, he was so happy. Later he started the "Baby Bird Project", a charity project aimed at helping disabled orphan infants and children in society — "Flying every hope with love".

"Every time I go to a charity organization, I bring a big truck full of diapers," said Mu Shengqiang, an operator of the company. "As long as he is in the company, President Wang will always help load and send the diapers. He really wants to do something to benefit children and puts a lot of time and energy into public welfare."

"We are creating a new domestic brand," Wang Shendi said, "and the first thing we should do is to have a good product and a sense of purpose. Doing charity can make entrepreneurship a happy thing."

Put 50% Budget Into R&D

Even though the company has passed through the initial start-up period, Wang Shengdi still maintains an invigorated state. Every morning after arriving at the company, he first checks in on the sales department. He then goes to the R&D department to track research progress, and then proceeds to the conference room to negotiate with suppliers. During this time he responds to any phone messages he may receive. In order to directly know the feedback of consumers and improve the product, he added his mobile phone number on the "Daddy's Choice" WeChat official account, and became the "chief customer service officer".

Staff member Mu Shengqiang told a story which vividly portrayed Wang Shengdi's personality. There was a time when Wang Shengdi was not satisfied with the product quality. He did not hesitate to destroy several truck loads of substandard products, valued at about two million yuan. He was very concentrated on maintaining high standards of his products, but he was quite careless about his own appearance. He had lost 15 kg, and his original woolen coat soon became too big for him, making it look like a big bag on his body. His pants had also become too big. "He did not look like the well-dressed overseas returnee! "

Nearly 50% of the company budget is spent on research and development. In the company's lab, there are samples of best-selling diapers from the United States and Japan. Wang leads the research and development team to constantly compare quality, to find the best material suppliers, and continuously test to strive for the best dry and comfortable absorption effect. Not surprisingly, as a result of all this work, the company has developed nine patents.

But what Wang is most proud of is that his company has created many jobs. He estimates that Daddy's Choice has nearly 10,000 stores, each of which employs two or three salespeople. His brand has therefore created more than 20,000 jobs.

"Entrepreneurs should have the confidence to change their field, and at the same time, they should keep innovating and create value for society." At the annual meeting of the Peking University Youth CEO Club where the up-and-coming generation came to "learn lessons" from Wang Shengdi, he shared his experiences with them, and told them to always "struggle without regret".

“便利侠”开创城市垃圾回收新模式

BLXIA Creates a New Model of Urban Waste Recycling

作者：王海涵　王　磊　刘晓朦
翻译：卢　敏

“便利侠”开创城市垃圾回收新模式

“丁零，您有新订单！”手机App发出提示后，“便利侠”们穿戴好统一的绿色制服，别上胸牌，佩戴好白手套，规划好同一区域订单的最便捷路线，按照约定时间驱车赶往居民家中回收废品。分类、称重、计算价格、打包运输，一系列流程麻利且专业，一般一单不会超过10分钟。

“家里空间有限，物品更新、淘汰速度快，直接丢掉又太可惜，自从有了‘便利侠’，我在网上预约，他们上门服务，获得的费用直接存进我个人账户，非常方便且环保。”合肥蜀山区居民李阿姨是“便利侠”团队的老客户了，她感慨，自从来了这群年轻人，小区很多居民都在家中主动把垃圾废品分好，再也不随处乱丢垃圾了。

“便利侠”是80后创业者邢卫创立的家庭废品一站式回收项目。邢卫毕业于一家985高校的电子与通信工程专业，从当年的IT学霸到当地小有名气的“破烂王”，邢卫和其团队一直致力于打造城市垃圾回收治理新模式，力图重新定义和制定相关行业标准。

“收破烂”绝不是“作秀”

毕业之后，邢卫曾在一家通信国企工作了十年。2014年，他决定离开这个外人眼中的“铁饭碗”岗位。“那时候，‘互联网+’概念特别火，很多行业都在尝试创新。我和合伙人经过详细考察，一致认为环保领域将迎来创业‘风口’，想趁着年轻奋斗一把。”

在他看来，收废品的人也许“玩不转”互联网，互联网创业者也可能“看不上”废品回收行业。因此，他下海创业、试水废品回收行业并非“作秀”，他认为一方面可以填补类似创业项目的空白，另一方面也想摘掉人们对废品回收行业的“有色眼镜”。

2015年，邢卫与合伙人拿着四处凑来的80万元正式成立公司“便利侠”。

他坦言，刚创业时，大家信心满满，一心想为废品回收行业注入互联网、信息化思维，树立新的行业标杆。然而，家人和朋友却抛出了质疑，他们觉得这个行业和年轻人“八竿子打不着”，哪有小年轻的蹬着三轮到处跑，和破烂儿、废品打交道？邢卫的父母虽然嘴上不反对，但是每个月都会问他：“这个月，你们工资能不能发出来呀？”

“过期药品、过期化妆品、纽扣电池、残留农药属于有害垃圾……纸的种类分为黄板纸、花纸、淋膜纸、白卡纸、铜版纸等。”那段时间，邢卫并未理会这些质疑，而是一心一意积累、学习环保相关知识，并亲自做市场调研，制定价格体系。

蹬过三轮、扛过家电

一开始，邢卫他们连捆废纸这个“基本功”都不会，经常刚下楼，一沓纸箱就散了，要拾掇半天。他为此专门去废品站请教，学会了正确的捆绑和绳索打结方法。

2016年，“便利侠”开通线上预约功

能，一旦收到用户订单，“回收小哥”就会上门分类回收塑料瓶、旧家电、金属等可回收物和有害垃圾；同时按照标准换算，给予居民储值积分。团队技术人员还搭建了线上商城，居民能用积分在此兑换垃圾袋、肥皂、毛巾等生活用品。

那段时间刚好是夏天，天气特别热。邢卫和合伙人每天早起，准备账本、绳子、秤、零钱等物品，接了订单就开始挨家挨户跑，热情服务，尽可能在有限的时间内推介自己的项目，给居民留下深刻印象。

“起初业绩一般。有的居民嫌预约、登记太麻烦，就直接把纸箱、塑料瓶丢给小区物业保洁。还有的老年人不会用手机，也不需要积分来兑换物品。”邢卫还记得，有一年自己生日那天，一位员工突然离职，其负责片区的垃圾没人收，他只好前去“顶岗”，爬上爬下搬家电，大冬天硬是累出一身汗。

团队坚持“一个瓶子也回收”的理念，服务半径没有限制。但是订单零散，预约时间也不均匀，再加上人手不充足，有时从市中心跑到郊区才完成两笔订单，运营成本居高不下。“创业起步阶段，我和合伙人蹬过三轮，用肩膀扛过家电、家具，也分拣过很多之前从未见过的塑料废品。说实话，这一行不好干。”邢卫回忆，干了一年多，团队的回收客单价一直提不上来，收支达不到平衡，大伙儿有些灰心丧气。

不过，他们终于看到了希望的曙光。2017年3月，国家发展改革委员会、住房和城乡建设部共同发布了《生活垃圾分类制度实施方案》，提出到2020年年底，要基本建立垃圾分类相关法律法规和标准体系，形成可复制、可推广的生活垃圾分类模式，并在46个城市实施生活垃圾强制分类，同时对生活垃圾的收集、运输、资源化利用和终端处置都提出具体规划。

垃圾分类再度成了社会热议的话题。

打通“最后200米”

“要再‘撑一撑’，接下来，人们的环保意识将逐步向节约、绿色转变，我们要利用垃圾分类推广契机，打造属于我们特有的废品回收模式和核心竞争力。"邢卫说。

2017年9月，他们经合肥市团委推荐，参加了中央电视台举办的《创业英雄汇》栏目；2018年5月，团队拿到第一笔来自专业投资机构的投资，开始思考服务模式的转型和升级，也尝试用大货车集中、定点运货和回收，将焦点集中在社区、小区的大体量订单，进行集约化管理、运营。

2019年，合肥市蜀山区相关部门向"便利侠"抛出了橄榄枝。此前，蜀山区就已经在合肥市率先启用"支付宝＋垃圾分类"智能回收平台，与"便利侠"合作后，由"便利侠"工作人员承担上门服务职能，串联起"线上＋线下"废品回收服务全链条。

"我们还增加了定时定点交投功能，提前收集小区、社区居民需求，在固定时间段，用准备好的大车集中收运废品，直接在网上结算、支付现金，解决居家废品回收的'最后200米'，这项服务覆盖了230个小区。"邢卫介绍。

随着订单量持续增长，"便利侠"在蜀山区陆续建立起25个社区分拣站，打造包括区级综合分拣中心、社区分拣站、小区定点回收服务、人员上门服务的四级服务平台。其中，社区分拣站的专业分拣员完成二次分拣，将废品送到区分拣中心进行细分、压包、粗加工，随后，将可回收物送去纸厂、铸造厂等进行重复再利用，将有害垃圾送到政府指定的处理厂，大大提高了工作效率。

每天在各个站点间穿梭是邢卫工作的常态。他和合伙人曾连续几周去一个小区参与具体工作，只为让居民熟悉自己的业务，提高参与度。

一些小区原本就有固定的收废品的人，邢卫决定不和他们构成竞争关系，“便利侠”吸纳废品站小老板进入分拣站工作，整合了资源。

经过三年的努力，“便利侠”终于实现了盈亏平衡。如今，越来越多的年轻人加入到“便利侠”队伍中，团队40余人平均年龄35岁，他们逐渐参与到城市治理的“大课题”中来，每天及时将各分拣站点的可回收物和有害垃圾数据收集、反馈给城管部门。“便利侠”还在货车车身喷涂垃圾分类知识，打造移动宣传阵地，并依托小区集中投放点和社区分拣站开展环保宣传活动，提高居民垃圾分类参与率。

2019年12月，“便利侠”获得团中央第九届“母亲河奖”绿色团队奖。“很多居民非常认可我们，知道货车几点来，都提前在小区里排队。”邢卫同时表示，由于废品的细分种类太繁杂，实现废品回收行业的标准化运作将是个漫长的过程。“但大伙有信心，继续创新工作模式，为垃圾分类、城市治理和环保宣传贡献更多智慧”。

BLXIA Creates a New Model of Urban Waste Recycling

"Ding Ding, you have a new order!"

The mobile app alerts employees at BLXIA (Convenient Waste Recycling Company) to put on their green uniforms, white gloves and their badges, plan the most convenient route for orders in the same area, and drive to clients' homes to recycle waste material at the appointed time. It is a series of swift and professional procedures including sorting, weighing, calculating prices, packing and transportation, and it generally takes no more than ten minutes for a single order.

"The space at home is limited, and things are replaced and fall into disuse quickly. It's a pity to throw them away. But because of BLXIA, I can make an appointment online and they'll come to my home to provide the recycling service. The value points are wired directly into my personal account, which is very convenient and environmentally friendly," said Li, a resident of Shushan District in the city of Hefei, Anhui Province, and a long-time customer of BLXIA. She said that since the company came to the community, many residents more actively sorted out their waste at home.

BLXIA is a one-stop household waste recycling project founded by entrepreneur Xing Wei. He graduated from a national key university majoring in electronics and telecommunications engineering. From an IT straight-A student to a well-known local waste recycling boss, he and his team have been committed to creating a new model of urban waste recycling and governance, trying to redefine and formulate relevant recycling standards.

Waste Recycling Is By No Means a Show

After graduation, Xing Wei worked in a state-owned telecommunications enterprise for ten years. In 2014, he decided to leave this secure job. "At that time, the concept of 'internet+' was particularly popular, and many industries were trying to innovate. Through detailed investigations, my partners and I agreed that the field of environmental protection would be a booming sector for entrepreneurship, and I wanted to do my utmost to found a start-up in this field while I was still young."

In his opinion, people who recycled waste material were not regular internet users, and most internet entrepreneurs did not pay attention to the waste recycling industry. Therefore, it was not a "show" that he resigned and started working in the waste recycling industry. On the one hand, there was a clear void in internet-savvy waste recycling companies, and he believed that he could fill this void. On the other hand, he also wanted to remove people's stereotype about the waste recycling industry.

In 2015, Xing Wei and his partners established BLXIA with 800,000 yuan raised from various sources.

He said that when he first started his business, everyone was confident and wanted to infuse modern methods utilizing the internet and information technology into the waste recycling industry to set a new industrial benchmark. However, his family members and friends raised doubts. They felt that this industry had nothing to do with young people. How can young people pedal three-wheeled carts around the city and recycle waste material? Although Xing Wei's parents had no objections, they asked him every month, "Can you pay your staff this month?"

"Expired medicine and cosmetics, button batteries, and residual pesticides are hazardous waste.... Paper is divided into strawboard, stained paper, PE-coated paper, ivory board, art printing paper, etc." At that time, Xing Wei did not listen to these concerns, but instead spent time and energy accumulating and learning environmental protection information, personally conducting market surveys and formulating a pricing system.

Pedaling Three-Wheeled Carts and Carrying Home Appliances

In the beginning, Xing Wei and the other employees didn't even know the basic methods of bundling waste paper. When they went downstairs after collecting waste material, a stack of cardboard boxes often fell apart, and it took a long time to clean them up. He went to the local waste material recycling station for advice and learned the correct binding and rope-binding methods.

In 2016, BLXIA launched its online appointment function. Once an order was received, recycling employees would come to classify and recycle plastic bottles, old home appliances, metals, other recyclables and hazardous waste. The items are valued according to certain pricing standards, and value points are given to the resident. Those points can then be used to "purchase" trash bags, soap, towels and other daily necessities from an online shopping mall set up by the team's technicians.

Basically speaking, BLXIA was paying people to recycle.

It was summer at that time, and it was extremely hot. But Xing Wei and his partners got up early every day to prepare the accounting books, ropes, scales, change and other things. After receiving the daily orders, they'd go out from door to door to recycle the items. They made it a point to be polite and cordial as they promoted their project. This left a deep impression on the residents.

"In the beginning, our business performance was mediocre. Some residents felt that it was too troublesome to make an appointment and register, so they just threw out their cardboard boxes and plastic bottles, which would be gathered by property sanitation workers in the community. Also, some elderly people didn't know how to use mobile phones and didn't need value points to get these daily necessities."

Xing Wei still remembered that on his birthday one year, an employee suddenly resigned, and the waste material in his area was not recycled. He had no choice but to quickly take his place. He rushed to the apartments to recycle the goods, climbing up and down the stairs to move home appliances. He sweated all through that winter.

The team adhered to the concept of "even a single bottle is recycled", and there was no limit to the service radius. However, orders started coming in from all over the city, appointment times were quite random, and they lacked manpower. Sometimes only two orders could be completed in a day traveling from downtown to the suburbs, and the operating costs remained high.

"In the initial stages, my partners and I pedaled three-wheeled carts, carried home appliances and furniture on our shoulders, and sorted out more plastic waste material than we had ever seen before. To tell you the truth, it was not easy to do," Xing Wei recalled. After more than a year, the team's unit price for recycling waste material could not be raised, and their profits could not match their overhead. Everyone was discouraged.

The next year, however, they finally saw rays of hope. In March 2017 the National Development and Reform Commission and the Ministry of Housing and Urban-Rural Development jointly issued the Implementation Plan for the Domestic Waste Sorting System. It proposed that by the end of 2020 a system of laws, regulations and standards related to domestic waste sorting would be formulated, and a domestic waste sorting model that could be replicated and promoted would be formed. Domestic waste mandatory classifications would be implemented in 46 cities. At the same time, specific plans were made for the collection, transportation, resource utilization and final disposal of domestic waste.

Waste sorting had become a hot topic once again.

Removing Waste Recycling Obstacles in the Last 200 Meters

Xing Wei told his employees, "We must keep working hard. The future will be that people will become more environmentally conscious and have a heightened awareness of green development. We must take advantage of promoting waste sorting to create our unique waste recycling model and core competitiveness."

In September 2017, recommended by the Hefei Municipal Youth League Committee, the team participated in the "We Are the Heroes for Entrepreneurship" program sponsored by CCTV. In May 2018, the team received the first sum of investment from a professional investment institution and began strategizing how to transform and upgrade their service model. They also started to use large trucks to gather, deliver and recycle waste material at fixed places, and also to focus on large-scale orders in communities to intensify management and operation.

In 2019, relevant departments of Shushan District in Hefei provided support to BLXIA. Prior to this, Shushan District had already taken the lead in launching the Alipay + Waste Sorting smart waste recycling platform in Hefei. This cooperation enabled BLXIA employees to go door-to-door and form the online + offline chain of waste recycling services.

"We also added the function of being able to schedule recycling waste material at fixed times and places, which allowed us to meet the needs of communities and residents according to the surveys we've made earlier," said Xing Wei. "We'd use large trucks to recycle and transport waste material at appointed times, and directly settle accounts online and pay cash. These were the final steps — or the 'last 200 meters'— in providing comprehensive domestic waste recycling services for the city. This service covers 230 communities."

BLXIA has established 25 community waste sorting stations in

Shushan District. This creates a four-level service platform, which includes district-level comprehensive waste sorting centers, community waste sorting stations, community waste recycling services at fixed places, and door-to-door services, of which professional sorters complete secondary sorting and deliver waste material to the district-level sorting centers for subdivision, pressing, and rough processing. After this process, the recyclables are transported to paper mills, foundries, etc. for reuse, and hazardous waste is transported to treatment plants designated by the government. This greatly improved work efficiency.

Every day, Xing Wei visits various waste recycling stations to inspect the work. He and his partners went to a community for several weeks to handle specific matters and help residents familiarize themselves with and participate in their business.

Some communities previously used to work with other waste collectors. Instead of competing with them, Xing Wei employed them to work in the sorting stations.

After three years of hard work BLXIA has finally broken even, and more and more young people are joining the team. There are more than 40 people on the team, with their average age around 35. They are participating in an important service within urban governance. Every day they gather data on recyclables and hazardous waste from various waste sorting stations and give feedback to relevant urban management departments.

The BLXIA trucks have also been designed with information about their services, creating a kind of mobile publicity platform. BLXIA also relies on community designated waste sorting places and community waste sorting stations to carry out environmental protection publicity activities which have enabled residents to take an active part in waste sorting. This is greatly beneficial in raising public awareness about BLXIA and waste recycling.

In December 2019, BLXIA won the Green Team Award at the 9th “Mother River Award” given by the Central Committee of the Communist Youth League of China (CYLC). “Many residents recognize our work very much,” Xing Wei said. “They queue up in the communities in advance, knowing when our trucks come.” At the same time, he also said that since the subdivision of waste material was so complicated, it would be a long process to realize the standardized operation of the waste recycling industry.

“But the team is confident, and we’ll continue to innovate the work model and contribute more to waste sorting, urban governance, and promote environmental protection.”

羊毛毡手作人在创业中逐梦

Wool Felt Craftswoman Pursues Her Entrepreneurship Dream

作者：魏旭平 朱娟娟
翻译：卢 敏

羊毛毡手作人在创业中逐梦

戴围巾的熊、翻白眼的驴、拿河豚手杖的娃娃……各式各样的手工艺品密密麻麻地站在一起，它们身旁躺着一团团五颜六色的羊毛。这是90后手作人苏芳工作台上的场景，制作羊毛毡手工是她的拿手绝活儿。

羊毛毡属于非编织而成的织品形式，具有良好的触感和还原性。羊毛毡手工就是利用羊毛毡材料制作玩偶、娃娃、杂货、配饰等手工作品，流行于欧美、日本等地，在国内还是个新鲜的手工门类。

成为独立手作人以来，苏芳摆过摊儿，开过工作室，放弃“赚快钱”，一心打造个人文创品牌，在创业中追求自己的梦想。

“做手工才是我想做的事情”

苏芳2012年从武汉科技大学城市学院环境艺术设计专业毕业。大学时期，她就对做手工情有独钟，“那时候我做过包包、衣服，还做过布艺、刺绣等”。

毕业后，工作一有闲暇，她仍然会进行自己的手工制作，看到好看的材料，她也总是悉数买下。

2014年6月1日，对苏芳来说是具有转折意义的一天。她请假到汉口天津路的爪哇酒吧参与了一次“蠢货市集”，见到了各式各样的手作人和手工作品。她不禁感慨：“原来做手工也能成为一份工作，这些人和我完全活在两个世界。”

因加班导致连续错过两期“蠢货市集”后，苏芳意识到自己的生活被繁忙的银行工作限制了。虽然收入不少，但“这不是我想要的生活状态”。她很清楚，做手工“才是自己想做的事情”。能不能把兴趣发展成职业？抱着试一试的想法，她瞒着家人辞去了工作，成为一名独立手作人，每天都在自己租的房子里做手工。

2016年，苏芳去了上海“1933老场坊”。第一次参加省外的市集，她带上了自己的作品——一批用羊毛毡加刺绣或羊毛毡加软陶做成的饰品。这些饰品吸引了一些年轻人的目光，不少人加了她的微信。同时，她也结识了一些从事文创行业的公司，并开展了部分合作。参加这样的市集不仅收获了信心，还让她了解到一些关于手工作品销售方面的知识，“那时候才懂得要根据工时和材料等方面来计算出作品的合适售价”。

随着眼界的不断开阔，武汉的手作市集已经无法满足苏芳学习的需要，于是她花着路费、交着展位费，隔三岔五到上海、广州、合肥、杭州等城市参加规模更大的市集。苏芳慢慢成了“圈里人”。

宠物定制类羊毛毡制作曾是一项主要业务

“沙沙沙……”指甲盖大小的一层羊毛，苏芳捏着戳针刺了百十下，终于让松散的羊毛变成紧致的“皮肤”，牢牢覆盖在内层骨架上。这样的工作，苏芳每天能在手工台上做近 10 个小时，“喜欢，所以一点儿不觉得枯燥”。

苏芳掸了掸手上的羊毛介绍说，羊毛

兼具柔软和坚韧的特点，纤维结构可紧密缠结；使用尖端有倒钩的戳针反复戳刺，可以使羊毛上的鳞片摩擦缠紧，变得结实。

出于对宠物的喜爱和对国外艺术家作品的欣赏，2017 年，苏芳开始学着用羊毛毡做宠物作品。因缺乏引路人，她的技术完全是自学的，没有教材，她就不断在网上找国外的书。

至今，苏芳还留有一本羊毛毡宠物猫作品介绍的日语教材。她对日语一窍不通，“不要紧，看着步骤图学呗”，苏芳反复操作，一点一点地摸索出制作技巧。刚开始练习时，不小心把手指戳出一个又一个血孔是常事，出于热爱，她常常忍着伤痛继续制作。

苏芳的第一个作品是两只小猫，发在朋友圈里被“很可爱”“很漂亮”这类的留言刷屏。可去年，她却因为觉得做得“不够好”，把这两个作品拆了，“我现在的作品和原来的作品差别很大，当时收到的评价都是‘好可爱’，我不想只得到这样的评价。”

渐渐上手后，宠物定制类羊毛毡制作成了苏芳的一项主要业务，顾客多为爱宠人士，大多希望苏芳能用羊毛毡来复原自己宠物的样子，用作纪念。在制作时，顾客会把自家宠物的生活照发给苏芳，并向苏芳讲述每张照片背后的故事，这也激发了她的创作灵感。

有一次，一名顾客在作品交付了一个多月后，用微信找到了她。那名顾客告诉苏芳，收到作品后不久，自己家的狗狗不幸出车祸去世了，每次看到苏芳的羊毛毡作品，就会勾起无限美好回忆。“顾客因有所纪念对我表示感谢，但在我的心里，正是因为这些故事，我觉得自己做的这些是有意义的。”苏芳说。

2017 年 11 月，苏芳在汉口租了一套房子创办自己的工作室。为了推广羊毛毡手工，她在工作室中低价开设教学课程，一堂课只收 20 元，还会备好材料。虽然不少人对羊毛毡手工感兴趣，但来上课的回头客几乎为零。

“许多顾客以为做羊毛毡手工很简单，不曾想要花几个小时坐在那里戳来戳去，根本坐不住，有时甚至会直接喊我帮他们代工。”苏芳说，“我觉得做东西认真是对它的尊重，顾客的表现让我觉得不开心。”一个多月后，她放弃了在工作室开课的想法，把时间全部花在自己的创作上。

“希望每个作品都是在兴奋的状态下完成的”

精进技术，不断超越自我，做出满意的作品，是苏芳做手工的初心。为了保持初心，苏芳一次又一次放弃了市场，因为她坚持“做手工不能和挣快钱完全画等号”。

2017年，她常驻武汉某大型手工市集，出售自己的手工作品。那时，供不应求是常有的事。周末，准备卖上两天的作品，到第一天下午就基本被抢购一空，好的时候，她一个月能卖1万多元。主办方要求摆满展台，她只能赶制一些简单又便宜的发卡、皮筋饰品来充数，有时她甚至故意报高作品价格好让它卖不出去，多在展台上留一会儿。“那时候，感觉自己就像是赶订单的流水线小工一样，虽然赚钱，但是学不到任何东西。”

苏芳说。

四处参加市集和展会的过程中，一些看中了羊毛毡手工商业价值的公司找到苏芳请求合作，希望能够用便宜的材料批量生产。“道不同”，苏芳都婉拒了。

“很多人做作品只追求视觉效果，所以选择偷懒，用不好的材料或偷工减料，导致作品很松软。但我的作品都是实打实的，也没有针孔。这没有别的办法，多花时间戳就好了。”在苏芳看来，“做作品就该老老实实的”。

前两年，羊毛毡宠物作品定制是苏芳的主要业务，占她收入的一大半。这项业务中，成交额最高的是一只全身定制的宠物狗，单价2000元。在她的微信通信录中，也有上百个好友是通过这一业务结识的。但苏芳觉得，定制业务像“命题作文”，个人创作灵感往往要向顾客的要求妥协，这使她丧失了一些对作品的热情。

久而久之，不开心的情绪渐渐强烈：如果继续做宠物作品，会比较容易挣钱，但创作灵感将受到限制；如果不做，短时间内，收入肯定会大降。2019年春节，苏芳一度很纠结。

最终，她选择了后者。

如今，苏芳与一名代理人合作销售现有作品。苏芳说："羊毛毡不同于流水线产品，不是布娃娃，它不仅精细程度更高、仿真效果更好，还包含着手作人的心血。几百元几千元的定价也不是随随便便喊出来的，要根据工序和材料计算成本得出。"她拿出最近制作的一只憨态可掬的"大灰狼"向记者举例，为了追求仿真度，狼的牙齿是软陶烧制的；骨架也选用进口的可塑性材料，因此四肢和尾巴都可以活动。这只"狼"是她与朋友合作的"小红帽"系列作品中的一个，作品工序复杂，制作精细，加上材料优质，定价在600元左右。

苏芳表示，羊毛毡作品仍然很小众化，很多人不理解一个作品中手作人付出的创意与心血，有时费了好大劲儿做成的作品，也有顾客很喜欢但觉得价高放弃购买。如今，她抱着"随缘"的心态卖作品，卖得出便卖，卖不出去就自己收藏，因为每一个作品都是她“在兴奋状态下创作出的挚爱”。

2019年5月，苏芳以800元卖出了一套原创的玩偶周边作品，包括帽子、装饰物等，这创造了她自主设计类作品成交额的最高纪录。

现在的苏芳过着“养得起自己”的生活，完全按自己的想法来创作，她感到很满足。她说：“生活与梦想之间总要有取舍，想要有所得，必然要放弃一些东西。”在创业的路上，苏芳成为了更好的自己。

Wool Felt Craftswoman Pursues Her Entrepreneurship Dream

A bear wearing a scarf, a donkey rolling his eyes, a doll holding a puffer fish cane…these were the handicrafts on the workbench of Su Fang, a twenty-something craftswoman. She made these handicrafts by hand in the middle of piles of colorful wool.

Wool felt is a non-woven fabric with good touch and elasticity. Wool felt material is used to make dolls, sundry goods, accessories and other handiworks. It is popular in Europe, the US, Japan and other places, and is still a new handicraft in China.

Su Fang turned away from making "quick money" and dedicated herself to becoming an independent craftswoman. In the beginning she set up stalls, but then eventually established her own studio. She has dedicated herself to forming her own personal brand, and continues to pursue her entrepreneurship dream.

"All I Want to Do Is Making Handicrafts"

In 2012, Su Fang graduated with a degree in Environmental Art Design from the City College of Wuhan University of Science and Technology. During her study at college, she had a special liking for handicrafts. "At that time, I made bags, clothes, cloth art, embroidery, etc."

After graduation she found work at a bank, but whenever she had free time she was busy making her own handiworks. When she saw beautiful material, she always bought it.

June 1, 2014 was a turning point for Su Fang. She took a leave of absence to participate in the handicraft market at the Java Bar on Tianjin Road, Hankou District, Wuhan City and saw all kinds of craftspeople and their handiworks. "I've discovered that making handicrafts could become a job," she recalled emotionally. "These people and I live in a different worlds."

Because of her busy work schedule at the bank, she lost two chances to participate in market craftwork events. She realized that her life was restricted by her busy bank work. Although her income was quite high, it was not the life she had wanted to live. She was certain that making handicrafts was what she wanted to do. She wondered whether she could develop her interest into a career. She decided to quit her job and try it. She didn't tell her family about her decision, and quietly became an independent craftswoman, making handiworks in her rented apartment every day.

In 2016, she went to Shanghai to participate in a market event outside Hubei Province for the first time. She brought her own handiworks — a batch of ornaments made of wool felt and embroidery or wool felt and polymer clay. These ornaments drew the attention of some young people, and many people added her WeChat information. At the same time, she also got acquainted with some companies working in the cultural and creative industries, and began to cooperate with them. Participating in the market event helped her not only gain confidence, but also become more familiar with the handiworks industry. Su Fang said, "At that time, I knew how to calculate the appropriate selling prices of handiworks based on working hours and material."

As she continued to broaden her horizons, the handiwork market in Wuhan could no longer be enough for Su Fang. She began traveling to other cities like Shanghai, Guangzhou, Hefei, Hangzhou where she'd set up her own booth and participate in larger fairs. Over time, Su Fang gradually became an insider.

Pet Handicrafts as a Major Business

Su Fang pinched a layer of wool the size of a fingernail and pierced it 100 times, finally turning the loose wool into a firm "skin" which covers the inner skeleton. She worked on the workbench nearly ten hours every day. "I like doing this, so I don't feel it's boring at all."

She brushed the wool on her hand, saying that wool was both soft and tough, and its fiber structure could be tightly tangled. Repeatedly piercing it with a barbed needle could make the wool more malleable and easier to work with.

Because of her love for pets and her appreciation of foreign handicrafts, in 2017 Su Fang began learning how to use wool felt to make pet figures. She had never had a teacher, so all of her skills had been self-taught. Without any Chinese teaching materials, she had relied on ordering foreign books through the internet.

One of her major sources of learning had been a Japanese textbook on wool felt cat works. She couldn't understand a word of Japanese. "It didn't matter," she said. "I just looked at the step diagrams and learned how to make them." After repeated practice, she gradually mastered the necessary skills. When she'd first started, she would accidentally poke bloody holes in her fingers. But because of her love for making craftworks, she endured the pain.

Su Fang's first pet work was a craftwork of two kittens, which were praised by friends as very cute and beautiful. But last year, she took apart the two works because she felt that they were not good enough. "My current works are quite different from those first ones. The comments I received at that time were 'very cute'. That was not what I was looking for."

Not long afterwards, making pet handicrafts became her main business. Customers were mostly pet lovers. Most of them requested that Su Fang make personalized wool felt figurines of their pets as souvenirs. Customers would send photos of their pets and tell her the stories behind each photo, which also aroused her creative inspiration.

Once, a customer contacted her one month after the finished work had been delivered. The customer told Su Fang that not long after she received the work, her dog died in a car accident. Every time she looked at Su Fang's wool felt work, it would evoke beautiful memories. "Customers thank me for such memories, but in my heart, it is because of these stories that I feel that what I have done is meaningful," she said.

In November 2017, she rented a place in Hankou where she created her own studio. To try to promote wool felt handicrafts, she offered training courses at a low price, only charging 20 RMB yuan per class, and she would also prepare necessary material. But although many people were interested in wool felt handicrafts, no one enrolled.

"Many people think making wool felt crafts by hand is very simple," Su Fang said. "They don't want to spend hours sitting and poking around. They cannot sit still, and sometimes people will even ask me to do the work for them. I think that spending time and energy in making something shows respect for it, and this attitude by people makes me very unhappy." After a month of no students, she gave up the idea of offering courses in her studio and spent all of her time on her own creations.

"I Hope Every Handiwork Is Completed in Excitement"

To improve her skills and constantly surpass herself while making quality handiworks has been Su Fang's consistent aspiration. To maintain that original aspiration, she gave up marketing time and again because, as she said, "Making handiworks cannot be about making a quick buck."

In 2017, she set up a long-term stall in a large handiwork fair in Wuhan to sell her own crafts. At that time, it was common for her supply to fall far short of demand. The handiworks she had prepared for the whole weekend would sell out by Saturday afternoon. When her business was brisk, she could make more than 10,000 yuan a month. The organizer told her to make more crafts, and she could only quickly make some simple and cheap hairpins and rubber band accessories to fill up her stall. Sometimes she had to raise the prices so that she wouldn't sell out and could stay in her stall for a longer period time. "At that time, I felt like a small assembly line worker who hurriedly finished orders. Although I was making money, I wasn't learning anything."

While participating in various fairs and exhibitions, she would meet companies that were interested in the commercial value of wool felt handiworks. They wanted to cooperate with Su Fang, hoping to mass produce her wares with cheap material. She declined as she believed, "Our goals are different."

"Many people only care about the appearance of the handiworks, so they do shoddy work and use inferior material, resulting in a softer product. But my handiworks are a result of hard work, and there are no pinholes. There is no other way than to spend more time poking them." In Su Fang's view, "Handiworks must be made honestly."

For two years, making customized pet wool felt crafts became Su Fang's main business, accounting for most of her income. Her highest priced item was a customized dog figure with a price of 2,000 yuan. Through her business, she became acquainted with hundreds of people through WeChat. But she felt that the customized business was restricting her personal creative inspiration, which often had to comply with the customer's requirements, which made her lose enthusiasm for work.

These unhappy emotions gradually became stronger. She knew that if she continued to make pet handiworks, it would be easy to make money, but her creative inspiration would be restricted. If she did not do this, her income would definitely drop in a short time. During the Spring Festival of 2019, she was torn between the two choices.

In the end, she made the second choice.

Now, Su Fang cooperated with an agent to sell her existing handiworks. "Wool felt crafts are different from products made from the assembly line. It's not a doll. It not only has a higher level of precision, but is also more lifelike. It's also made through a craftswoman's hard work. The price of several hundred yuan or several thousand yuan is not randomly set. The cost should be calculated according to the handicraft process and the material."

She took out the figure of a sweet timberwolf which she made recently and showed it to reporters. To get the right look, the wolf's teeth were made of polymer clay, and its skeleton was imported plastic material so that its limbs and tail could move. This wolf was one of the handiworks in the Little Red Riding Hood series made through cooperation with her friend. The handiwork was exquisite, and the material was high-quality, so its price was fixed at about 600 yuan.

Su Fang said that only a small number of customers were interested in wool felt handiworks. Many people did not understand the creativity and painstaking efforts of the craftswoman. Sometimes a customer could appreciate a handiwork made through great efforts, but felt that the price was too high, and so would not buy it. She did not feel pressure now to sell her handiworks. If she failed to sell them, she would hold onto them, because each one she made was created with passion.

In May 2019, she sold a set of doll handiworks including hats, ornaments, etc. for 800 yuan, which created the highest transaction record of her independently designed handiworks.

Now that she had the means to support herself, she could create her handicrafts according to her own ideas and felt more satisfied. "There is always a choice between living your life and living a dream. If you want to get something, you must give up something."

On the path to starting a business, Su Fang has become her better self.

出 版 人：王君校
策划编辑：刘小琳
责任编辑：杨　晗
英文编辑：韩芙芸
封面设计：袁长新
排　　版：北京几何创想艺术设计有限公司
印刷监制：汪　洋

图书在版编目（CIP）数据
创业者：幸福是奋斗出来的：英汉对照／“最美中国人”丛书编委会编著．-- 北京：华语教学出版社，2021.11
（最美中国人）
ISBN 978-7-5138-2194-0

Ⅰ．①创… Ⅱ．①最… Ⅲ．①人物—先进事迹—中国—现代 Ⅳ．① K820.7

中国版本图书馆 CIP 数据核字（2021）第 185520 号

创业者：幸福是奋斗出来的

“最美中国人”丛书编委会 编著

*

华语教学出版社有限责任公司出版
（中国北京百万庄大街 24 号　邮政编码 100037）
电话：(86)10-68320585, 68997826
传真：(86)10-68997826, 68326333
网址：www.sinolingua.com.cn
电子信箱：hyjx@sinolingua.com.cn
北京虎彩文化传播有限公司印刷
2022 年（16 开）第 1 版
2023 年第 1 版第 3 次印刷
（汉英）
ISBN 978-7-5138-2194-0
006900